Wm. McGonagall Poet.

NO USELESS TROUSER ENCIRCLED HIS GROIN
 BUT IN BONNET AND TIGHTS WE FOUND HIM
AND HE STOOD LIKE A MODEST TOBACCONIST SIGN
 WITH HIS TARTAN CURTAIN AROUND HIM.

𝔇𝔢𝔡𝔦𝔠𝔞𝔱𝔢𝔡 𝔱𝔬 ℌ𝔦𝔪𝔰𝔢𝔩𝔣, knowing none greater.

This is
The Book of the Lamentations
of the
Poet Macgonagall

Portraying in his own Unapproachable Style his Birth and Parentage, Early Struggles, Miraculous and Hairbreadth Escapes, with a Graphic and Characteristic Account setting forth how, by his Inspired Genius and Indomitable Pluck, he passed from Penury and Persecution through a Knighthood into an Immortality of Fame.

O'er all the Bards together put
   From Friockheim to Japan,
He towers above, beyond dispute,
   Creation's greatest man.
Prize Poem,

The Robe of his Inspiration
A Unique *Mantle*piece.

CONTENTS.

Chapter		Page
I.	I AM BORN	5
II.	THE GENIUS OF POETRY VISITS ME	11
III.	MY FIRST INSPIRED WORK	20
IV.	I AM INITIATED INTO THE ORDER OF THE BATH AND RECEIVE A CHEQUE	32
V.	A CHAPTER OF ATROCITIES	40
VI.	I PROCEED ON FOOT TO INTERVIEW THE QUEEN AT BALMORAL	47
VII.	I GO TO LONDON	55
VIII.	I GO TO NEW YORK	68
IX.	I TAKE GLASGOW BY STORM	81
X.	FAREWELL FOR EVER TO DUNDEE	90
XI.	I GO TO PERTH AND VISIT INVERNESS	100
XII.	I AM MADE A KNIGHT OF THE WHITE ELEPHANT OF BURMAH	112
XIII.	I GO TO EDINBURGH	123
XIV.	THE POET ATTENDS HIS OWN FUNERAL	134

THE BOOK OF THE LAMENTATIONS OF THE POET MACGONAGALL.

CHAPTER I.

I AM BORN.

> Rejoice, Edina, shout and sing,
>   And bless your lucky fates;
> Macgonagall, the lyric king,
>   Was born within your gates.—*Delhi Thug.*

Place of my birth. LIKE most great men I was born at a very early period of my existence, in that oderiferous portion of the globe, yclept the Grassmarket of Edinburgh—sacred to the memory of Burke and Hare and the rest of the Covenanters. These Covenanters I have always held in the highest esteem, striving as they did at the risk of their lives in the best interests of Presbyterianism and medical science. A lot of them slew James Sharp, who opposed the progress of the former, and Burke administered the same drastic remedy to daft Jamie in order that a fuller knowledge of anatomy, through Knox and his confreres, might be given to the world.

Though quite a number of them passed away in the place where I was born, I never felt impelled by the muses to celebrate their taking off. Such subjects seem to have attracted Burns in a very especial manner, as witness that rollicking, boisterous and characteristic ditty of his, setting forth the unseemly levity displayed at his own execution by that ferocious fiddling felon, McPherson, the freebooter, so called, I understand, from his persistent practice of acquiring his footgear in the absence of the shoemaker.

I have always prided myself on approaching such themes with the reverence which they demand, an attribute which was conspicuous by its absence in "Rantin' Rhymin' Robin."

But to resume.—The Grassmarket, as every reader of history knows, has from time immemorial been a prolific outlet to those places to which the bell invited the soul of the good king Duncan, was in fact an arena, which until my advent was more celebrated for its public exits than its private entrances. These exits—at least those of them which bulked most largely in the public eye—were made either to the rhyming of Lady Macbeth's Knell or to the other place according to the taste and fancy of the spectator.

Reminiscences of the place of my nativity.

I am bound, however, to admit that a considerable majority of his audience saw in imagination the indomitable spirit of my famous countryman already alluded to, the senior partner of that well-known firm in the West Port,

"Glide unpitied to that zone
Where drink and skating are unknown."

But history plays such fantastic tricks we never know how the next generation will view such startling events. I have no doubt that even at the time—and without waiting for the verdict of posterity, Burke had had his sympathisers at that grim show, and the sincere regrets of many learned men, who now found themselves in the position of Napoleon at St Helena, or his nephew at Chiselhurst—*without subjects*. Only once, so far as I can gather, was there complete unanimity in the Grassmarket as to the direction taken by the principal performer.

This was in the case of John Porteous, Captain of the Edinburgh town guard, whose victims neither went to swell his own purse nor advance the interests of science, and who for such wanton waste of material, was at the last moment of his existence initiated by the mob into the ancient order of the "Diers" on a pole specially stolen for the purpose.

Historical incident in the Grassmarket.

Good heavens! A murderer hanged by thieves!! Could any place be disfigured by deeper degradation than this?

Is there any purging process or panecea known to scientists or theologians which could sweeten such a damned spot? Could any good thing ever after come out of such a Nazareth? Aye, gentle reader, there could. An event happened which not only condoned the piled-up iniquity of the Grassmarket, but threw a radiance of everlasting glory over it. It was the birth of a poet, right opposite the very place where that dyer's pole stood.

My birth condones the iniquity of my birthplace.

You have seen a puddle of mud on a pavement, which, approaching, you, if a lady, gathered up your skirts to avoid. There were many such in the "Pends" and "Closes" of the classical spot where I first saw the light. But these self-same puddles, full of contamination, acted upon by the sun, left the filth behind, and carried the pure rain drops, of which they were mostly composed, right up to the blue ether, to bless and fructify the parched land in due season. In like manner so shone the sun of genius in the mire of my humble surroundings, and enabled me in after years to pour out blessings on all mankind; blessings which, I am sorry to remark, have up till now been repaid only by visions of future fame and the sterner realities of fierce famine. Were it not that history changes so much, and that the outstanding characters in it are so kaleidoscopic, I would long ago have lost heart altogether, given up the hungry battle, and returned once more to carpet weaving. But I know that the world's recognition will come. What I am concerned about is—Will it come in time for me to eat of its fruits, drink of its delights, and be couched on its beds of down?

Hope in historical changes.

Alas! alas! it sometimes takes three hundred years to put these things right. Our Dichty Water neighbour, John Graham of Claverhouse, was once a fiend incarnate, who drank a cup of Covenanter's blood every morning to breakfast; and John Brown of Priesthill was an angel of light and wisdom. All this is now changed. It has been discovered that the two John's were sixty miles apart when the one shot the other with a horse pistol, that Claverhouse was a perfect gentleman and a high-souled patriot, and that John Brown, if he ever was shot, richly deserved it, because, rather than pray for the poor misguided King, he would leave his wife and weans widowed and fatherless.

Instance of historical change.

Speaking for myself, and with all due reverence, rather than lose a shirt button under the same circumstances, I would pray for the devil himself, or even the magistrates of Dundee, who forced me to quit the city. In the land of my fathers those who went armed agin' the Government were not called Covenanters but Fenians, and when they did their last dance on nothing it was merely justice, not martyrdom. I wonder what Skin the Goat will be a hundred years hence.

Only one true Covenanter living now.

As far as I know there is only one true Covenanter living now, and all his brethren of the cloth sneer at him and persecute him, even as the men of this generation persecute me. Some of them here have even had the audacity to call him " A regular M'Gonagall," a compliment to his steadfastness, intended in their own ignorance to insult him, and cover up their own backsliding ; for it is beyond question that these men, the descendants and successors of the true blue sons of the Covenant, are now perpetuating in their churches exactly what their fathers died to abolish, and are thus more eloquently than in words sneering at the sacrifice of their martyred sires,

Courage, Jacob! the children of this generation will not always be wiser than the children of light, who will yet place both you and I on top.

Another instance of reversed history.

But another instance of the freaks of history and I am done as far as this is concerned. I have heard that it is the custom amongst some of the South Sea savages to prostrate themselves in adoration before a select group of their wooden deities in the forenoon of their Sabbath. In the afternoon they get a shot at them for its equivalent in cowrie shells for a penny. My authority for this is a sailor friend of mine called Tim O'Brien, and whether it is actually the case or not, the same mixed up state of things occur with us every day, only the transitions may not be quite so sudden.

The Scottish people, for example, are popularly supposed to venerate the memories of the good and godly elders of, and subsequent to, the Covenanting times, and yet to-day these worthy men are resurrected from their tombs, and trotted out on the stage of a theatre, by shrewd Scottish authors for the double and successful purpose of making their descendants laugh and filling their own capacious pockets. I do not say that this is either right or wrong. I have no great feeling on the matter as far as that aspect of the case is concerned; all that I want to point out is the change, and to argue from it, that though my work is unappreciated now, it is no stretch of the imagination to say that I may be working for the appreciation of a wiser generation yet to come.

This is the only excuse I have to offer for this historical digression from my birth, boyhood, and parentage, which I will now resume in the next chapter of this remarkable book.

CHAPTER II.

THE GENIUS OF POETRY VISITS ME.

> The spae wife lookit at him sair,
>   "Oh, wonderous strange," she cried,
> "Title and genius plainly there
>   With poverty allied."—*Poetical Horoscope.*

IT was the Grassmarket, then, which was the place of my birth, and the arena of such stirring events as I have already indicated. I am most particular in reiterating and emphasising the fact, because of the many discussions which invariably succeed the demise of eminent men as to the exact spot of their nativity, as well as its local colouring and odour.

This remarkable event took place all unheralded some seventy-odd years ago. My parents were poor but bibulous, the one circumstance contributing largely to the other. That they were intelligent to a degree goes without saying, since I, their sole surviving and orphan son, by a strange and eclectic natural process have had conserved in my own colossal cranium the best parts of both, the baser instincts having been eliminated by the sheer force of the *perverfidum ingenium Scotorum* which I, though a Milesian on both sides of the house, possess in a much higher degree than that terribly over-praised and far more immoral than immortal Burns.

Character of my male progenitor.

My male parent was undoubtedly a man of great capacity. He could carry his besetting infirmity well, it evidently having as little effect on his venerable carcase as castor oil on a graven image. He was no classical scholar however, neither was he a profound theologian, inasmuch as he never could be made to understand the difference between "*meum* and *teum*;" while his hazy and indistinct views with regard to the eighth commandment frequently led him into unsatisfactory debates with a gentleman in a horse hair wig, which usually terminated in the question being referred to some dozen uninterested spectators, who almost invariably recommended the retirement of my venerated sire from the arena of discussion for periods varying from 4 to 14 weeks. With these trifling exceptions, the moral character of the elder M'Gonagall was fairly passable, and calls for no further notice in this veracious history.

My boyhood.

Strange as it may appear, my boyhood was principally remarkable from the fact that nothing remarkable developed itself in me, beefsteaks and poetical visions being alike strangers on my path. Still, like ordinary mortals, I plodded upwards and onwards, until I at length arrived at a manhood quite as prosaic as that of the Directors of the Newport Railway, who in after life refused me a perpetual pass. Poetical portents may have illumined the horizon, Eolian harps may have sung in sweet and weird-like symphonies that the lyre of Apollo was soon to be struck by a master hand. Forerunners and precursors may have sighed in every breeze, fluttered in every leaf, and swelled from the throats of all the feathered warblers; but I knew it not, for the goddess of poetry still stubbornly refused to unlock her mighty secret even to me. Prosaically, therefore, I courted, prosaically I married, and begat sons and daughters without anything anywhere to indicate the slumbering volcano of genius which lay hid in the recesses of my placid breast.

By this time I had migrated to Dundee after vicissitudes too horrible to recapitulate. Here I learned the trade of carpet weaving, and here also I developed an ardent love of the drama, especially the plays of Shakespeare, which in due course I could act, as my great chum and ardent admirer, Michael Kinchley, used to declare, as well as the great author himself. The knowledge of this acquisition was soon bruited abroad, and was (as well as myself) taken every advantage of, Giles, Forrest Knowles, McGivern, Johnnie Woods, and others of like kidney filling their wooden temples of Thespis from floor to ceiling whenever I was billed to appear. The filling process, however, stopped there, and rarely reached either my purse or my stomach. But I liked the work, and was glad of the practice—not of acting for a bob a night—but of qualifying me for Drury Lane, which was now the goal of my ambition. Yes, my friends, I became a great actor and a great playwright long before I totally eclipsed these magnificent accomplishments in the realms of poetry.

I come to Dundee and learn carpet weaving.

Managers hear of my powers as an actor.

I have often wondered whether the world is most indebted to Dundee or Edinburgh in this respect; whether the palm should be awarded to the place of my birth, without which, of course, I could never have been, or to the place of my histrionic and poetical awakening, without which I never might have been either a poet or a carpet weaver. Goodness knows! Sometimes I wish I had never been born, sometimes I wish I had never seen Dundee, and sometimes a good square meal has reconciled me to things as they are. Edinburgh, with the exception of the Magistrates and student portion of it, was far from kind to me; the Dundee Magistrates were positively brutal, and prohibited my performances in any of the public places of amusement, while for me to walk up any of its streets and meet one of its jute mills coming out was simply to court annihilation deliberately. And yet for the sake of one good Dundee gentleman I could forgive Dundee for much. This was a well-known reverend gentleman, between whom and myself a warm friendship sprung up, which lasted till his death. Every Friday evening found me at the manse declaiming the works of Shakespeare in a manner which he always pronounced perfect.

My treatment in Dundee and Edinburgh.

There was another warm supporter of mine in Dundee —a burly man of iron, who stuck to me through thick and thin, but who now, alas, is also dead. To show how ardently he took my part, it is on record that a certain civic dignatory in the city once expressed his astonishment that a man of my friend's attainments could waste his time listening to what he was pleased to call "the drivel of a poor fool like M'Gonagall." My champion, bristling up in wrath, replied, "Sir, I am not astonished at your astonishment; your life is one continual round of drivel, and poor M'Gonagall would be no change at all to you." This man of iron was a poet of no mean calibre, and it is unnecessary to add that my daily communings with him at length created in me

I find a noble champion.

a strong desire to emulate his attainments in the domain of verse. I tried hard, but my effusions were miserably poor, until at length I gave it up in despair. My patron seeing evidence of splendid rhyming abilities persuaded me to renew the attempt. I did so, and, fortunately, I have two or three specimens of the amended productions—still uninspired—which are interesting, as showing the uselessness of any one trying to write verse without being called upon to do so by the genius of poetry. And here I may state for the edification of those who peruse this unique volume that I endeavoured at this time to produce a Tay Bridge poem, but which, like the first Tay Bridge itself, was a miserable failure. The first stanza will possibly be as much as you can stand.

My first attempts at poetry.

My first Tay Bridge poem.

"The Tay Bridge is a beautiful span,
And the river Tay runs through it;
A wonderful work by the hands of man,
Many strangers come for to view it."

My faithful friend and critic condemned it right off, so I tried my hand at a love song—my very first verse:—

"As I was a-passing yon valley so sweet,
A pretty fair maid I chanced for to meet;
Her step was so light and her gait was so free,
I ne'er loved a woman as well's I loved she."

The marked difference between this and my more matured "Bonnie broon haired lassie o' Dundee," I leave my readers to note. I next tried my hand at descriptive verse, choosing Glasgow for a subject:—

"I've travelled this wide world over,
And many a river beside;
But the prettiest river that ever I saw
Was Glasgow, on the Clyde."

rather fancied this myself, but it was also ruthlessly and inexorably condemned, with the assertion that in all three instances the grammar was faulty, as if, forsooth! (so I thought at the time) I could allow any minor consideration of this sort to interfere with the clinking of the lines, which, after ?", is the chief difficulty of the poet. The most adverse critic I ever encountered subsequent to my inspiration frankly admitted that "my clinking or rhyming was unique." The only cruel and unfair thing he said was, that before I reached that point, I had "to defy grammar and murder common-sense." This envy-begotten tirade would have vexed me very much prior to the entrance of the genius into my humble dwelling; as it was, it only amused me, and perfectly paralysed him when I calmly asked him "Whether he or the genius from whom every line I now wrote was miraculously communicated knew best what true poetry was?" With tears of regret in his eyes, he shook me warmly by the hand, gave me twopence for a penny poem, and asked me to call at his address with my succeeding effusions.

My first adverse critic.

And now, gentle reader, I imagine I have gradually prepared you for a description of what was possibly the greatest event of the 19th century. I refer to the visit of the genius of poetry, who had not appeared in Scotland for over 100 years. On that occasion she was the guest of Robert Burns. Where she had been and what she had been

The greatest event of the 19th century.

doing during this long interval there is no means of ever knowing. We have no evidence that Scott or Byron ever saw her. My theory is that Scott was too much of a "hybrid," and that Byron, accustomed as he was to such surreptitious visits, had possibly seen, but mistaken her identity. Of course, the same suspicion might as easily have attached itself to Burns, only from his account of the interview he was dead tired that night with thrashing, had just partaken of a very meagre supper, was evidently in a mood wholly inconsistent with his usual "Willie-brewed-a-peck-o'-maut" vein, and growling over the condition of his "Sark" to the music of the rats in the riggin'. So that, on the whole, we may safely assume that his narrative of the vision were the words of soberness as well as of truth.

Burns' account reliable.

If such surroundings as Burns describes conduces to the appearance of the genius, God knows I completely filled the bill on that, to me, most miserable, and yet most happy day. A day or two before my most esteemed friend had given me a cast-off suit. I was wearing this suit on the day in question. My memory is clear on the subject, for I had no other. The day was the Monday of the Dundee Fair of 1877. It was a bright summer's day towards the end of leafy June.

Circumstantial account of the visitation.

The rest of the family had gone their several ways of enjoyment; ways of enjoyment which amply bear out the truth of heredity, inasmuch as from the oldest to the youngest, irrespective of age or sex, they adhered religiously in their recreations to the transmitted predelictions of their venerable grandsire, intermitted in one generation. This was the reason there was absolutely nothing in the house in Paton's Lane in which I sat clothed in the good man's garb, hungry, penniless, and altogether unutterably miserable. The bright sun and waving trees mocked and augmented the poignancy of my grief until my waking mind could bear the strain no longer, and, sinking back in my chair, I resigned myself to a drowsy, dreamy condition, which completely stole over my senses.

Full description of the appearance of the genius. Presently I felt a delightful sensation of heat all around the soles of my feet, which increased so much in intensity that I started up, wide awake, amazed at the peculiar feeling. By and bye, in circling sinuosities, like the twining of a warm snake, the strange like caloric percolated upwards, and encircled my loins as with a girdle. Pausing there for a brief space, and filling my wondering soul with never-to-be forgotten awe, it speedily monopolised my entire frame, which anon glowed like a furnace. On looking towards the roof, midway between it and my head, right in the middle of the room, and suspended in space, a hand holding a quill pen appeared, and a voice cried three times distinctly and audibly, Write! Write!! Write!! and on looking once more I saw a shadowy form

Graphic description of the vision continued. draped diaphanously holding a scroll of music in its hand. That this was the genius of poetry I had not now the slightest doubt; that I had received my commission there could be no room for the smallest question; but still the problem to be solved was, What should I write?

All at once the inspiration by a process peculiarly its own directed my attention to the garments I wore, then vanished, voice and pen, and all. Like a thunder clap the theme dawned upon me as the name "Gilfillan" rose involuntary to my lips. And here I must pause a brief space to elucidate

The genius gives me a subject.

my theory with regard to inspiration—a theory which has been so amply confirmed in my experience, that it has ceased to become one.

This inspiration always comes in heat, and when it never rises higher than the knees it is still there, but the inspired one can only write in such a case regarding feats of walking, running, &c. When it reaches the heart an intense desire to write love songs supervenes, such as my "Bonnie broon haired lassie." When it seats itself in the loins and arms in equal proportions, love and fighting find meet expression in such productions as "The Rattling Boy from Dublin town." When the breast, arms, legs, and head are all aglow war songs are the dreadful issue; but on this the date of its first visitation, the head and heart alone being most palpalably affected, the genius called to me in accents I could no longer misunderstand to write in praise of some man great in head and heart; but whether the wearing of the clothes suggested the theme, or even incited the genius to visit me at all, I leave for future generations to wrangle over. Suffice it to say, I wrote a poem that same afternoon in his praise, and without signing any name to it, put it into the letter box at the *Weekly News* office, and anxiously awaited the result— a result which, along with the poem, my first inspired work, will appear in the next chapter.

My theory of inspiration.

CHAPTER III.

My First Inspired Work.

Ower a the bards together put,
From Friockheim to Japan,
He towers above, beyond dispute,
Creation's greatest man.—*Prize poem.*

My first inspired production, WITH what eager avidity I unfolded the ensuing Saturday's sheet, and with what tears of joy I read my first inspired production *in extenso* can be better imagined than described; and to add to the full cup of my ecstatic delight the Editor appended the remark that "this contribution to the literature of the 19th century was evidently the work of a modest genius, who was unwarrantably hiding his light under a bushel." As it marks such an important epoch in my literary career, I here give this much praised poem in full.

" All hail to the Rev. George Gilfillan of Dundee,
He is the greatest preacher I ever did hear or see;
He preaches in a plain, straightforward way,
And people flock to hear him night and day,
Because he is the greatest preacher of the present day.
The first time I heard him was in the Kinnaird Hall,
Lecturing on Garibaldi as loud as he could bawl.
He is a charitable gentleman to the poor while in distress,
And for his kindness unto them the Lord will surely bless.
My blessings on his lofty form and on his noble head;
May all good angels guard while living, and hereafter when dead."

Contemporary criticism.

The "Birkie Gazette and Liff Romancer," in a lengthy review of this poem, which it published without leave first obtained, says:—"An appreciative poem by a new author has recently appeared in the columns of a contemporary. We make no apology for giving it to our readers. Had it been conceived and couched in the ordinary society journal style, or been the work of some over-praised darling of the salons of Edinburgh or London, we might have paused before laying ourselves open to the charge of an infringement of journalistic etiquette by publishing it without leave. But when we inform our readers that a most unaccountably serious omission in reference to a work of this calibre has been made in the neglect to copyright it; that, as a tragedian, his performances were long ago favourably criticised by us when he starred at Giles' and Johnnie Wood's, and that since its first appearance in the columns of our contemporary we have become possessed of a copy of the poem in question for the sum of one penny, which we had the honour of placing in the hands of the gifted author himself. When all this is taken into consideration the matter assumes a different complexion, and turns what otherwise would have been a grave and unwarrantable breach of the friendly relations which have so long subsisted between us and the *Weekly News* into a positive benefit both to that newspaper and the poet.

"In the first place, we advertise, reiterate, and emphasise the fact that the undivided honour of its first appearance belongs entirely to that paper, and at the same time brings more forcibly under the notice of the reading public, that the talented actor once lived and weaved carpets in the adjoining community of Lochee, and that now having placed his hand to the plough of poetry he may be expected very soon to burst out in a fresh place."

"This poem," 'The Gazette and Romancer' goes on to say, "is the first inspired work of the author, and speaks for itself in words more eloquent than we can employ. It is short, but all embracive. It commences with the orthodox Hail! the reverential greeting accorded to Macbeth by the weird sisters. Still following the lines of Shakespeare, our bard gives the saluted hero's place of residence. He of Avon, though not more accurate in this respect, was possibly more prophetic, and sets down not only Macbeth's cognomen and present location, but the names of other two or three places to which, all unknown to himself, he was expected soon to flit. This, as we before remarked, is less the province of the poet than the prophet, and therefore in no way detracts from the performance of Mr M'Gonagall, who we understand, as yet at least, lays no claim to the mantle of Elijah."

Great thoughts strike great minds in the same way.

Possibly this is what the Editor refers to when he says I may be expected to burst out in a fresh place. That up till this time I was not among the *profits* is painfully apparent. But to resume, the Editor concludes by a trenchant analysis thus :—"The rest of the poem is taken up with the power of his subject as a preacher, the manner of his preaching, his appreciation by the people as evidenced by their attendance by 'night and day,' when the author first heard him, his subject at that time, the strength of his voice, his kindness to the poor while he was in distress, what his reward will be ; and lastly, that splendid invocation which is the gem of a piece, which will live as long as his fame as a tragedian, and is of itself proof positive of a special commission."

The lasting nature of my poetry.

My next, and in many respects greatest effort, was my Tay Bridge effusion. This beautiful poem, which was the means of giving me first rank as a poet, was written under considerable difficulty, as we shall see presently. Happening to be in the house on the occasion of this, the second visit of the "divine afflatus," I seized a pencil and scrap of paper, and, spreading out on my knees a pair of bellows, began to write vigorously. I had only got the first stanza three parts completed when in rushed my infuriated and unsympathetic spouse, and, seizing hold of my improvised desk, began to belabour me most unmercifully. Fearing that the inspiration might cool down, I stayed not to retaliate or even to remonstrate, but, rushing wildly from the house, I made for the first open door, and there I finished in aromatic peace that piece which has since so astonished the literary world, and of which my friend Gilfillan said, "Shakespeare never wrote anything like this," which I have always looked upon as the greatest compliment I have ever received.

(margin: I attain first rank as a poet.)

I would liked to have given you this grand effort in full, but since the fall of that ill-fated structure in 1879 I made a solemn vow to destroy every copy I could come across, and never publish it again. So anxious was I to become possessed of copies of this poem for cremation purposes that I actually on one occasion, besides its original cost of a penny, offered a man "A Rattling Boy," a "Bonnie broon haired lassie," and two "Silvery Moons" for it, but in vain. He said "he would never part with it," although he was far from being a wealthy man, but would get it framed, and keep it for ever." Had I not been so overjoyed at such appreciative devotion I would have felt angry at the man; as it was, I gave him a "Rattling Boy"

(margin: Flattering appreciation by the man in the street.)

at half price, he having no more on him. I have never seen him again, and possibly never will; but for the ray of light and hope he that day shed on my hungry soul, may he live till he pays me that halfpenny.

The poet without honour in his own city.

The effect of those two poems on the public was brilliant but transitory. For a space Professors, doctors, lawyers, and clergymen were numbered in my extensive clientile. As soon as a fresh effusion emanated from my prolific brain, I made my rounds all over the city. You ask me why I did not get rich? Alas, dear reader, as a rule I never got more than a penny from each patient. Some of them occasionally gave me threepence when they had no coppers, and on rare occasions I have got as much as sixpence. These sixpences, however, were as rare as angels' visits, and many of the givers of them would remind me at the next call, when I laid down the new poem, that "that was other four I was yet due them." I was once nearly losing one of these *rara avises*—a regular sixpence every time contributor—but managed after some trouble to retain him. It was in this wise: A clergyman in the country, whom I had long reckoned as one of my most ardent admirers, on one occasion returned me my poem with a letter, without enclosing his customary sixpence. The letter ran as follows:—

My diplomacy.

DEAR MR M'GONAGALL,—I herewith return the poem you posted me. I have been thinking over the matter, and now blame myself for encouraging you by my contributions to waste your time at this sort of thing, instead of working at some useful occupation. I understand you learned carpet weaving, and was at one time regularly employed at this useful craft. Take my advice, and return to it; write your poems in your leisure hours, and send me copies as heretofore, and I will continue my donations. Otherwise send me no more of them. Believe me, I have nothing but your own welfare at heart in advising you thus.—Yours truly, ———.

A poet's righteous rage. Imagine, if you possibly can, the tempestuous passion into which the receipt of this monstrous epistle threw me. I raved and stormed like an infuriated maniac; a she bear robbed of her whelps was placid calmness to my raging wrath. I neither ate nor slept for twelve hours after its receipt at 5 P.M., but paraded the bounds of my single apartment like a caged hyena. Gradually calming down, I fervently invoked the aid of the genius, and replied thus:—

Dear Sir,—Yours to hand. The poet is superior to the divine, and gives, does not take advice. The counsel you proffer to me is exceedingly applicable to yourself and to most of your brethren. Paul was possibly as good a preacher as any of you, and yet he worked during the week at tent making, simply because it does not require the same amount of application to make a sermon as it does to compose a poem. Had he been a poet there would have been no tent making. That is the great difference between your calling and mine. I have no doubt that, although you engaged in shoemaking all the week, and preached to your flock on Sunday, the majority of them would be quite satisfied, so long as you did not preach long enough to weary them or loud enough to keep them awake. My audience is the world, and not a small section of a community who come to hear you from force of habit, listen listlessly, and forthwith forget. I have put my hand to the plough of poetry, and no mundane occupation or consideration of any kind shall ever distract my thoughts from the mission so solemnly entrusted to me. Hoping to hear from you with usual enclosure.—I am, yours truly,

WILLIAM MACGONAGALL, Poet.

I got another letter from the tenacious gentleman, in which—to make a long story short—he pointed out at some length the difference between the circumstances and capacity of the apostle, myself, and the writer, and concluded by reiterating his former advice; to which I replied :—

> Dear Sir,—This correspondence must cease. It is Coin I want, not counsel; unless, therefore, I get *that* by return, I will hand all the letters to the newspapers for publication.— Yours truly,   WM. MACGONAGALL, Poet.

By return I received six stamps, which I speedily converted into half a loaf and half a pound of cheese, which I and my family ate with triumphant satisfaction. But, my powers considered, things did not turn out financially anything like so well as I expected, and they grew worse. My source of income was both limited and precarious; in fact, during all my career as a duly inspired poet my remuneration, far from being in accordance with my merits, never even reached the level of my needs, calculated on the humblest scale. Turning out hundreds of poems on all conceivable subjects, I could not flatter myself that I was cultivating the muses on even assured oatmeal. Nothing seemed certain to me but disappointments and cold water, to the latter of which I rigidly adhered after the following occurrence. Some so-called friends of mine, in recognition of the honour reflected on the district by the event of the visitation, invited me to a commemoration banquet in Lochee.

The utter insufficiency of my earnings.

I am invited to a banquet,

Habited, as specially requested, in the garb of my annunciation, I presented myself in due time at the feast, which, to tell the truth, was to me a perfect revelation of good things. I was received with an acclamation in every way satisfactory. In due course the chairman, evidently much affected, requested me to stand up. I did so, then all the rest, chairman included, knelt around me on their knees, and broke out into a mighty shout of "Long live the Prince of poetry, the great and glorious M'Gonagall."

An affecting spectacle. I was mightily affected as the audience rose to their feet, and took their seats with adoration clearly written on each face. The chairman then announced that, as a fitting and solemn sequel to this sublime spectacular effect, he had a toast to propose, and he hoped that every man present would see to it that his glass was fully charged in order that it should be drunk with all the honours "in a clean coup up and nae heel taps." This was received with a roar of applause which nearly lifted the roof, and when asked if I would have a tumbler of toddy or a glass of whisky, I emphatically replied,

I announce my temperance principles. "No, gentlemen, I am a strict teetotaller, and if I drink anything at all it will be a bottle of lemonade." This was instantly forthcoming and set down already decanted in a huge tumbler by the obliging and courteous waiter at my back.

"Now, gentlemen," cried the chairman, swinging his own aloft, "are your glasses charged? One foot on your chairs, please, and the other on the table. Here's to Scotland's immortal and inspired poet, the great M'Gonagall. Hip, hip, hurrah!" In a moment their glasses were drained, in another the well-known strains of "He's a jolly good fellow" were given over and over again with such power and effect as to be heard half a mile away.

On quietness being restored, I was called upon to respond, which I did in my usual modest and effective manner. I began by thanking the gentlemen present for the honour they had done me, related minutely and with great acceptance the story of the visitation, and stated, as my connection with Lochee was of so close and intimate a nature, the honour of the advent of the genius was an honour reflected on them individually and collectively, and concluded by proposing the healths of the whole company, to which—though only in lemonade—I would drink as heartily as I had just seen them do to mine; then, amid renewed thunders of applause, I drained my glass to the dregs.

Now, whether it was the mention of the name of the "Genius,' the flush of conscious and appreciated greatness, the closeness of the atmosphere, the odour of the tobacco smoke, or the fumes of the toddy around me, I know not; but I felt a peculiarly pleasant exhilaration pervading my brain, such as I had not experienced since the mantle of poetry descended upon me. The feeling in every respect seemed to be exactly the same as on that memorable occasion. In fact, such was my exaltation of soul and power of utterance that never in the whole course of my existence had I rendered my "Bannockburn," which I was called upon to recite, with anything like the dramatic power and thrilling effect with which it was given on this occasion.

As soon as I had finished, another lemonade was handed to me, which I enjoyed immensely. After this I gave the "Rattling Boy" with such verve and vigour that even I, who have electrified delighted audiences with it a hundred times and with comparative equanimity, was com-

I sing my favourite song,

pletely carried away with the swing and rush of my own voice. I gesticulated like one inspired, a condition by this time I felt almost certain I was in. There was the self-same dry, parched sensation about the roof of the mouth—a peculiar feeling, which made a third lemonade very refreshing indeed.

By this time I required no persuasion to sing, recite, or make speeches, which dazzled me as well as the audience with their lurid and burning eloquence. I was happy, but thirsty; but as the supply of aerated water was evidently unlimited, and the quality all that could be desired, the dry, crackled feeling in my mouth was never allowed to continue long. Anon I began to feel an inclination to embrace every one who came near me, and on the waiter setting my last drink on the table from behind, the tears of gratitude welled from my eyes, and I turned and blessed him with a subdued pathos, which greatly affected the courteous, honest, and kindly old fellow.

Ultimately, being asked to propose a vote of thanks to the chairman, I rose very cautiously for this purpose, and looking towards the chair I distinctly saw two occupants therein, on which I exclaimed, "There are more Richmonds in the field than one," and turning round in a paroxysm of coughing, the tears streaming from my eyes, I staggered to the place recently occupied by my chair, and collapsed on the floor completely "hors de combat."

A humiliating position for a poet,

I learned all this afterwards, for next day, when I awoke to consciousness with my cheek skinned, my knee bruised, and found my wallet with my manuscripts gone, I firmly believed I had been poisoned at the instigation of some jealous rival; but the doctor who was called

—to my utter surprise and horror—diagnosed the case as a simple drunk, and prescribed the taking of a blue pill and the pledge. I took them both, and kept the latter. About mid-day, when I was able to move, I rose and found my inspiration coat like the county of Cromarty, abounding in detached portions, at which I wept copiously, and at once proceeded in righteous wrath to Lochee.

I called on the chairman, a most respectable and respected man, who for the past fifty years has been prominent in every good work connected with the dark suburb, and entering his shop tattered and seedy as I was, I struck my best tragic attitude, and belched forth in anger and anguish, "Who steals my purse steals trash; 'tis something, nothing, 'twas mine, 'tis his, and has been slaves to thousands; but he who filches from me my good name robs me of that which not enricheth him, but makes me poor indeed."

I quote Shakespeare to some purpose,

"What's like the maiter wi' ye, poet?" he questioned urbanely. "Have ye lost anything?"

"Oh, no," I answered with all the irony and sarcasm I could muster, "Solomon says 'A good name is better than riches.' Shakespeare copies and endorses the sentiment, but I question if either of them ever dreamed of such an experience as I passed through last night. I was robbed of my means of livelihood—my precious wallet, my senses and my self-respect were stolen, my good name was filched from me, and all at one fell swoop, and you ask me if I have lost anything. I have lost everything, sir; but like poor, blind Samson—who also was made the sport of the Philistines—I will have my revenge, and pull your temple of Dagon on the top of you all, though I myself should perish in its ruins."

To do the man justice, he exhibited no guilty feeling, but bore my black and scrutinising looks, my uplifted stick, and my fierce denunciations without flinching, and calmly assured me in unmistakable accents of sincerity and truth that he knew nothing whatever of the vile whisky-drugging plot, and imagined until lately that I was drinking undiluted lemonade every time. He also told me that it took him from 11 P.M. till half-past one next morning to convey me from the Albert Hotel, where the affair took place, to my home in Paton's Lane, and as he had to carry me all the way, his only surprise was that I was not more severely battered, as on four or five occasions I slipped over his shoulder on to the hard, frosty road, his sole reward at the end of the journey being a fearful tirade of abuse from my justly indignant spouse. But as he sympathised with me to the extent of a new coat and a few shillings, I forgave him freely, convinced he had nothing to do with the matter except acting as chairman to a pack of blackguards, and the good Samaritan to me.

Although I too was altogether blameless, and the victim of a plot as senseless as it was diabolical, it almost cost me the friendship of one who had often kept my soul and body together, as we will see in the next chapter.

CHAPTER IV.

I am Initiated into the Order of the Bath and receive a Cheque

> Oh, had he lived 'mong ancient Greeks
>   He wad been crooned wi' laurels;
> Instead of wearin' cast-off breeks,
>   And livin' on dry farls.—*Prize Poem.*

I CALLED on the gentleman referred to in my last chapter, expecting sympathy and solatium; but before I had time to open my mouth he called me a drunken beast, having evidently heard of the Lochee exploit. "Sir," I cried, losing my temper, "You are a liar, and that is strong language for a poet to use." "Clear out," he retorted, "and don't call here again." For three weeks I did not, and was very miserable in consequence. At the end of that time a mutual friend gladdened me with the news that Mr So-and-So was anxious to see me in order to apologise.

I am forced to use strong language.

I hastened to his place of business at the shore, and, approaching him with a half bashful confidence, said, "I understand, sir, you are prepared to apologise for calling me a drunken beast."

"I am, poet," he frankly rejoined, "When I called you by that dreadful name, believe me I meant the opposite of the reverse."

"Thank you, sir," I replied, "I can see now that it was only the want of ignorance on your part, and I am fully satisfied with your apology," and tendering my hand with a smile, something entered the palm of it with the feeling of a red hot needle. On looking I saw it was a copper tack, and foaming with righteous rage, I at once rushed at him with my stick uplifted, when he cried vehemently, "Hold, poet, hold. I am woefully disappointed in you. I was reading this morning that General Grant, and, in fact, all great Generals, were always coolest on the point of attack, and resolved first opportunity to see if great poets were the same. Unfortunately, I see they are not, and I am more sorry than you can imagine."

Calming at once, and seeing the point, I told my friend —whom I was very anxious to conciliate—that he should have given me due warning, and I would have stood it like a martyr; then stretching forth my hand with the mein of a spartan under torture, I said "Try it again, please, and I'll not flinch a single inch." But here the incident closed without further experiment, and that tack after all, instead of causing more bloodshed, only rivetted our friendship closer.

In a previous part of this history I mentioned the fact that before I became great in the realms of verse I had written one or two pieces for the stage. These are still in their virgin purity, not one of them having yet been acted. My "magnus opus" in this direction is a manuscript which took me six months to compose, and nearly half that time to write out. It is a tragedy of the Shakespearean type, and is entitled "Jack o' the Cudgel," in seven acts. I tried to keep it in the legitimate bounds of

I am a playwright as well as a poet.

five acts, but became so intensely absorbed in my subject that the end of act five was reached with barely half of my characters killed.

In this dilemma what was I to do? Two modes of procedure presented themselves. I could re-write it in a condensed form, which would enable me to dispose of my heroes and heroines with less talk and more action; or I could let the plot run to its natural conclusion irrespective of its length, and allow the party to whom I sold it to cut it down to suit himself, or make two plays of it for that part, so long as I got my money for it. This course I eventually decided to adopt, entirely for the reason that, so well pleased was I with its contents and general arrangement, that I could not bring myself to alter a single syllable.

It is simply perfect in phraseology, balance, design, plot, and general excellence, so I finished it, and carefully put it past as a source of income if I happened to fall on evil times. It is, in fact, my reserve fund. So long as I stuck to the loom no serious evil times came; they waited till I began to write poetry, which would not sell. The genius impelled me to write, but she had evidently no control over the sales department; and so on one occasion, when the larder had been empty longer than usual, I took my manuscript of "Jock o' the Cudgel" to Mr Hodges, the genial manager of Her Majesty's Theatre in Dundee, to get it valued. He advised me, if I wished to sell it, not to part with it for less than £100. I thanked him, and departed to seek a merchant.

My unique reserve fund.

Some one, I forget whom, told me that a good actor, a fellow-countryman of my own, Gardner Coyne by name, was that week appearing at Johnnie Wood's theatre in the

Seagate, and that he thought, as Gardner had plenty of coin, and was raising a company of his own, he would be a likely buyer. To Johnnie's theatre, therefore, my manuscript like a little family Bible under my arm, I accordingly hied, and found my prospective customer and his wife the sole occupants of the little brick building. After introducing myself with my best stage bow, salaaming three times to the lady, I tapped the tragedy under my arm with the forefinger of my right, and asked if he was in the market for a play as good as any of Shakespeare's. He smiled a little, and asked me to leave it with him till next day, and he would give me an offer for it if it suited. It was a fearful risk, and I did not sleep that night, for I had left it with him without any security. On presenting myself next day, he said "I have looked through your tragedy, and am prepared to give you half a crown for it." At first I thought he meant to pay me that sum for the look he had had at it; but as soon as he made it apparent to my astonished ears and senses that he meant his thirty dirty coppers to be the purchase price of it right off, I faced him like a lion, and wrenching my precious document from his hands, shouted in the hearing of his wife and one or two smiling "toffs," "Sir, if that tragedy was boiled in muck you would not get a spoonful of the broth for half a crown."

My courtesy and politeness to a lady.

"Don't get in a passion, my man," he coolly replied, evidently anxious to turn the tables and score before his friends, who were now laughing like to split, "if you refuse my offer the matter is ended, and no great harm done; but, I say, look here, I have the manuscript of a good Irish song. How could we swap? What difference would you take between them?"

"Go, sir," I thundered, "and ask the Directors of the North British Railway Company what difference they would take between a box of matches and the Tay Bridge." And so shouting, I hurried off. If my precious tragedy was worth no more than the valuation this man put on it, God help me. I would in that case have nothing more to fall back upon in distress than a straw mattress in a dingy garret. But I have it yet; my faith in it is still intact, and unless I can find a purchaser who is able to talk something like reason, I would like it buried with me in my coffin.

Failing to dispose of it, I wended my way to Paton's Lane, and instead of partaking of what my poor stomach so urgently craved, I tried to forget its pangs in the melancholy task of looking over the piles of my unsold poems. Alas, I thought, as I gazed at them in despair, instead of an inspired poet, I am more like a manufacturing chemist, for of late everything I have turned out has been a drug on the market; a reverie which was rudely interrupted by my prosaic and practical spouse, who shouted out "What's the use o' moligruntin' there, Willie; tak' awa' twa or three hunder o' thae 'poms,' as ye ca' them, and see if ye canna get onything fae the grocer for them, for rowin' tobacco in."

I am liker a chemist than a poet.

Roused to action by this ridiculous suggestion, I donned a long surtout and lum hat which I had got the day before from a draper in Reform Street, and sallied out with a big bundle of my poems and songs under my arm, little thinking of how soon and in what a wholesale manner they were destined to be disposed of. As I wended my way townwards I saw three young men standing at the door of the Young Men's Club at the Nethergate end of Tay Street, and the thought at once struck me that here was my chance for a big sale, for this institution, originated and kept up by Mr Armitstead, M.P., was the resort of hundreds of young men of the better sort, who were fond of literature of the right kind.

Approaching the young men, I asked if they were in want of anything in my line. "O, yes," said one of them; "come this way, Mr M'Gonagall." With high hopes I accompanied the three of them into what appeared to me to be (and what I afterwards had no doubt about) a bathroom. When all four of us had entered the door was shut, and in a twinking I was in that bath, with the silk hat and poems floating around me, and the young men gone. Hatless and dripping as I was, I rushed up Tay Street, and in the words of my Bannockburn poem, describing King Edward's flight, "never halted till I reached Dunbar," who in my case, however, was Mr Dunbar, the Fiscal, whose office was in Bell Street. He at once despatched two policemen to investigate.

On arrival with me they were told by the caretaker that he had seen no young men about the Club that morning. "This," I shouted, "is a conspiracy to defeat the ends of justice. You are conniving at their escape. I tell you these young blackguards must be got, and made to pay the price of my hat and poems, and if the policemen do not apprehend you I will charge them with neglect of duty." My passionate, all-round accusation made things worse, for the caretaker boldly asserted that I had thrown the poems into the bath myself in order to obtain damages, and had pitched the hat in beside them to strengthen my claim, while the policemen peremptorily ordered me home.

I defy and indict all and sundry.

By this time the rim had been cut off my hat and my poems rolled into a ball of pulp, showing that the young blackguards had re-appeared on the scene of action during my absence at the Fiscal's. I had, therefore, no other course open than to make my way home hatless and wet, to find a flutter of excitement reigning in my domestic circle. A letter had arrived with a cheque for £5 from an anonymous admirer. It was drawn on the Dundee Banking Company, and was accompanied by a letter giving instructions for me before presenting it to get it endorsed by the parish minister. By this time it was too late, as the banks were shut, and Dr Watson's house at the Glebe too far away. I managed, however, to borrow five shillings on the strength of it from a neighbour, the Michael Kinchley already alluded to in these pages. With this we had a burst—the first for a long time—of ham and eggs. My initiation into the order of the bath was speedily forgotten, and joyous hilarity—so long a stranger to me and mine—reigned unrestrainedly. I cried in the exuberance of a full stomach. "Surely we have come to the turning of the lane at last, and peace and plenty will ever after be the order of the day in this house."

Early next morning, accompanied by my friend Michael, I set out for the manse. Arrived there, I rung the bell, and we were shown in. The good doctor—evidently in a bad humour—looked first at the cheque and then at me, saying, "I am afraid there's something wrong here. The bank is unknown to me, and even if it had been, if the cheque is all right, I do not see what use my signature would be."

"Oh, sir," I said, "the bank is all right, for I have seen it in Commercial Street, between the Murraygate and Seagate."

"That may be, but if the cheque is in order, and the bank all right, you do not need me to sign it. Good morning." He then disappeared, and the servant showed us to the door.

"I don't like this," said Michael, as we reached the Ferry Road, "and I am beginning to think that the burst last night was at my expense."

I said nothing, but as I knew the bank well, having sold many a poem in it, I was far from despairing. We arrived at Commercial Street about eleven o'clock, and found the bank right enough, but it was shut. I knocked at the door several times, but there was no response. As we stood on the pavement gazing up at the sign, Michael sneering, and I still hopeful, a little, thin, dark cadaverous hunchback came along. I asked him when the bank would open. In a voice I will never forget, he croaked in a manner which reminded me of Poe's raven, as he answered "Never more," and passed on. Then Michael opened his mouth and blasphemed. He did more: he accused me of **I am accused of forgery.** filling up that cheque myself in order to get his five bob advance on it. These two comparatively innocent stages past, he struck me on the mouth with his clenched fist, and I knocked him down with my stick. A crowd gathered, a policeman came, and but for that policeman being one of my admirers, Paton's Lane would not have seen me again for probably thirty days.

CHAPTER V.

A Chapter of Atrocities.

> And such a yell was there,
> Of sudden and portentous birth,
> As if men fought upon the earth,
> And fiends in upper air.—"*Sir Walter Scott.*"

BY this time—having had to give up selling on the streets as positively dangerous to life and limb—I had done fairly well in the shops, but as soon as the foregoing episodes got noised abroad a change came over the attitude of this section of my clients. To do them justice, it was the assistants, in the absence of their principals, who first initiated the discord. My best business was done generally amongst grocers, who often, in addition to the legitimate price of the poetry, would hand me a piece of well-matured cheese or a blown tin of beef to carry home with me.

Well do I remember the first time the demon of discord was let loose. It was in a grocer's shop in the Hawkhill, during the absence of the "boss" through illness. I was politely asked into the back shop for the purpose of exhibiting my latest production. No sooner had I unslung my wallet, and laid some dozen or so of them for inspection on a soap box, than the air was literally darkened with volleys of spilt oranges, rotten apples, and putrid eggs, which burst on my devoted head with the force and precision of hand grenades. My natural impulse was to attack, stick in hand, but my first rush at the foe was the last; my improvised counter, the soap box, gave way in front of me, I falling

I fight against fearful odds.

prostrate over it, hurting myself severely with protruding nails. From this unromantic position I was rudely revived by a torrent of water from a hose, which played impartially all over me. In my blind retreat to evade this I backed into the open hatchway, and fell into the cellar, which, fortunately for me, was not many feet from the shop floor, and plentifully furnished with straw. On this I lay dazed for a few moments, then gathered myself together, and proceeded in haste to the police office, where I was coolly informed by the Lieutenant on duty that "they really could not be annoyed any more with me and my complaints."

Methinks I hear some of my readers remark, "There's not very much in this." I quite agree with you that, unfortunately for me, there is nothing new in it; but it was true all the same, and marks another important departure in my career. A new and more exciting use had been found for me in shops which I was not prepared to contribute to, and my feud with the authorities had entered a more acute stage. One apprentice told his fellows of the great "fun" they had had with the poet, that the police would not interfere on his behalf, with the result that within a week, in almost every provision shop in the city, every rotten egg and orange, aye, even dead cats, were carefully stored up ready for my appearance on the scene. I had, therefore, to walk wisely or suffer, and my choice lay between hunger and bruised bones. Like a famished mouse, I often approached the trap and sniffed at the roasted cheese, knowing perfectly well the doom that awaited me if I dared to nibble, yet often impelled to try again. It was of no avail; every time I tried to take the bait and leave the hook I was had, and so, not wishing to become a martyr before my time, I at length resolved to avoid shops altogether.

Fortune at this time favoured me by an introduction to Baron Zeigler, who ran a variety entertainment at the old circus at the back of the Queen's Hotel. I told him of my quandary without reserve. He sympathised, and offered me a week's engagement as a trial at a reasonable figure. It did, indeed, prove a trial to both of us. The first night I appeared there certainly was a little undue excitement amongst the audience, and some throwing of objectionable and dangerous missiles; but on the whole I was allowed to proceed in comparative peace with my famous "Bannockburn," which was applauded to the echo. Next night, however—shall I ever forget it? Never! I shall carry its memory as well as its marks to the grave. Until that night I never for a moment imagined that there were so many veritable fiends in all Europe, let alone Dundee. To understand the proceedings thoroughly, it is necessary to give you a slight idea of the geographical bearings and general construction of the building.

I am introduced to a Baron.

Being formerly used as a circus, it is almost unnecessary to premise that the interior was round. The stage projected into the ring from the east end in the shape of a three-quarter circle, round which, some four feet below, the orchestra was seated. Directly in front, and facing the stage, with their backs to the west, sat the sixpenny ticket-holders. On the north was the fourpenny seats, packed like herrings in a barrel from floor to ceiling; and on the south, directly across the platform, were the two and three shilling chairs, more or less comfortably filled. Between the fourpenny and the two shilling seats ran the shilling promenade, the floor of which was the roof of the entrance to the stage for the performers. It was from this elevated "coign of vantage" that the unrehearsed proceedings started.

As soon as I emerged from under it, and had just reached the platform, arrayed in my Celtic garb, with sword and buckler complete, strutting as proud as a peacock, a whole big jute bag full of soot was emptied right over me. I would have turned and fled, but the little Baron was behind me shoving me forward with his stick, and shouting "Don't be a coward, M'Gonagall. Let the devils see there's pluck in you yet. If you show the white feather now, by G— they'll wreck the bloomin' place in 'arf a mo." Thus urged, I walked boldly forward to the far end of the stage, and had only time to say in tones of mortal anguish, "Gentlemen," when an unparalleled atrocity occurred. Boots, beef tins, rotten eggs, and bricks showered around me, and with such force were they hurled that such of them as missed me ricochetted from the platform right into the plush chairs beyond; one navvy's boot catching a white haired old gentleman right in the jaw, and flooring him completely. From this place a general stampede took place, the orchestra finding safety for themselves and their instruments below the scene of action. They were lucky, for the mad rush of the chair-holders over the sixpenny seats between them and the door led to a general engagement, and many went down in that awful melee.

A suitable oblation.

All this time the batteries from the fourpenny side—far from being silenced—were keeping up a brisk fusilade, having, I imagine, succeeded in procuring a fresh supply of ammunition, a portion of which, in the shape of a huge brick, at length caught me right in the stomach, when, like "Abner, dean of angels,"

"I smiled a sickly kind o' smile,
And curled up on the floor,
And the subsequent proceedings
Interested me no more."

I afterwards learned that the Baron, under cover of a huge umbrella, rescued me from the scene of action, and brought me partially round in the dressing-room. If ever man deserved a Victoria Cross for saving life under fire, that man was the redoubtable Baron. My condition, as you can guess, as I limped home leaning on Michael Kinchley's arm, was far from an enviable one. Poor Michael, who supported me manfully and tenderly all the way, and in perfect silence, except once, when he halted to dislodge about a pound of soot from my chest. Then I heard him mutter sympathetically that his uncle had been through all the Crimean War and the Indian Mutiny, "an' hidna gotten half as muckle as you've gotten this nicht, Willie." I remarked that the Baron deserved the Victoria Cross; did he get it? No! what he did get was an intimation next day from the magistrates of Dundee that if ever M'Gonagall took part in any of his entertainments again his licence would at once be withdrawn.

A plucky rescue.

What a pitiful exhibition of utter feebleness, imbecility, and injustice was here displayed. The wrong-doers were let off, and those who tried at the risk of their lives to preserve the peace were punished—the one with a threat to deprive him of his daily bread, and the other practically sentenced, without trial or inquiry, to starvation, after being half murdered, and wholly buried in soot. "Oh, wise Daniels come to judgment." This, then, was the melancholy predicament I had at length reached; the man in the street had failed me, the shops were impossible, and the public places of amusement peremptorily prohibited. The question I had now to settle was—Will I give up Dundee or the

A terrible predicament.

poetry? How I longed for light and leading. And it came in the shape of a copy of the "Delhi Thug," sent direct from India by an old admirer of mine, who left Dundee many years ago, and is now sub-editor of that highly cultured paper. In a letter accompanying this paper my friend wrote:—

> In a previous issue, which I cannot at the moment lay hands on, a splendid compliment was paid to one of your songs. The notice, so far as I can remember, ran something like this:
>
> "Dundee, it appears to us, in the matter of song appreciation, is very far back. M'Gonagall lives there, and we understand he is far from wealthy. A foreign gentleman, a distinguished ornament in the musical world, in a letter to us, pays this splendid and pathetic tribute to one of this talented, but neglected, bard's beautiful songs: 'I have heard,' he says, 'in a cathedral in St. Petersburg, aided with the soul-calming scenic effects of elaborately stained windows and flower-decorated aisles, the glorious strains of the "Messiah" by a thousand performers.
>
> 'At Berlin, on the occasion of a great Imperial "fete" in the august presence of the Emperor and Empress, I have heard the "Watch on the Rhine" on golden harps and silver trumpets. I have drank in with raptured ears the telling vocal strains of the "Marseillaise" by moonlight. Have, in fact, heard every musical effect from that produced from the Indian tom-tom right up to the great organ of St. Paul's, and wedded to the sweetest words, both secular and divine; but the most enchanting and harmonised blend that ever vibrated through the inner recesses of my grateful soul was M'Gonagall's "Rattling Boy" to the homely, but effective strains of a butcher's mincing machine.'"

Put that in your pipes, ye Dundee scoffers, and smoke it. "Richard's himself again!" I may, nay will leave Dundee; but after such consolation as this, never will I desert the muses.

Sir Garnet's astonishment.

In the same letter my friend adds—"Fancy that, poet, and picture to yourself the utter astonishment of Sir Garnet Wolseley when sent by the Government to annex the Fiji Islands, and on calling for a native song, to be regaled by one of the mahogany chiefs with "The bonnie broon haired lassie," and to be told that the negotiations could go no farther unless a clause was inserted that M'Gonagall's poetry —the only British literature known in these islands—should henceforth be admitted duty free."

Oh, Dundee, Dundee! "how often would I have gathered"—but I am afraid you are past redemption.

CHAPTER VI.

I Proceed on Foot to Interview the Queen at Balmoral.

> Our gracious Queen a pleasure missed,
>   'Twas well she did not know it;
> For Royal hand was never kissed
>   By such a famous poet.—"*Anonymous.*"

ABOUT this time the Newport Railway was completed, and in due time the theme caught my fancy; but the question which confronted me was—Where would I dispose of it? the ordinary channels being closed against me. But the peons of praise as recorded at the end of last chapter were so highly pitched and so greedily appreciated that I resolved to risk it, and trust for an abundant outlet in the magazines. It is a most moral poem, and can be read with perfect safety in the most religious household. In fact, no Young Men's Christian Association should be without it. For use in schools—if properly used—it is worth a guinea a copy.

I write a moral poem for the magazines.

And yet, "Tell it not in Gath," I offered this valuable contribution, which contains not a single immoral line or prurient suggestion, to the *British Messenger*, the *Gospel Trumpet*, and the *Christian Treasury*, by all of whom in succession it was "declined with thanks."

I then offered it, along with the copyright, to the Directors of the North British Railway, telling them that I had been credibly informed that, but for this descriptive masterpiece, that railway would have been one of the most disastrous investments of modern times; but there was no answer, either with or without an enclosure: I asked them for a perpetual pass over it, but with the same silent and non-committal result.

My Newport Railway poem. It may not be entirely out of place, as marking the full extent of this railway ingratitude, to give this beautiful descriptive poem in its entirety here:—

Success to the Newport Railway,
Along the braes of the silvery Tay,
And to Dundee straightway,
Across the bridge of the silvery Tay,
Which was opened on the 12th of May
In the year of our Lord 1879;
Which will clear all expenses in a very short time:

Because the thrifty wives of Newport
To Dundee will often resort,
Which will be to them profit and sport,
By bringing cheap tea, bread, and jam;
And also some of Lipton's ham,
Which will make their hearts feel light and gay,
And cause them for to bless the opening day
Of the Newport Railway.

The train is most beautiful to be seen,
With its long white curling cloud of steam
As the train passes on her way
Along the bonnie braes of the silvery Tay.

And if the people of Dundee
Should feel inclined to have a spree,
I am sure 'twill fill their hearts with glee
By crossing over to Newport;
And there can have excellent sport,
By viewing the scenery beautiful and gay,
During the live long summer day.

And then they can return at night,
With spirits light and gay,
By the Newport Railway
By night or by day,
Across the railway bridge of the silvery Tay.

Success to the undertakers of the Newport Railway;
Hoping the Lord will their labours repay,
And prove a blessing to the people
For many a long day,
That lives near by Newport,
On the bonnie braes o' the silvery Tay.

Discerning public, kindly judge betwixt them and me. Poor Homer, singing and begging through the seven cities, who afterwards quarrelled as to which of them he belonged, how thy melancholy fate depresses and yet cheers me—depresses me to note the poor rewards the contemporary generation bestows on genius—and cheers me to think that it *was* genius which was so treated after all.

I have often wondered if Homer was simply neglected by the men of his time. If so, comparatively happy, oh, ancient minstrel, wert thou, for thy grievances in such a case were simply of a negative kind. Mine, I grieve to say, are of a more positive character, as wounds and bruises and rotten eggs can testify.

I have never been devoured by wild beasts at Ephesus, or any other place; but this, apart, I question if the apostle was, "taking it all in all" (as the immortal William says) ever half so harrassed as I have been.

Starvation, my chronic condition, aggravated by offerings of gallows buttons for medals, pelted with pease, rotten apples, treacle, flour, and all sorts of abominable and unmentionable offal. Lord, such a life I have led. Such a horrible reward for a blameless soul, throbbing with heaven-born genius. The curses of all the poets, from Homer downwards, seem to have settled on and abidden in me.

Curses fall on my devoted head..

I have written scores of times to Her Most Gracious Majesty the Queen, have addressed Gladstone, Wolseley, and all the other "big bugs" in the land, and have waited in vain for enclosured answers with a deferred hope, which has nearly driven me sane. At length I resolved to call on Her Majesty personally, all other resources here having failed. No sooner was this resolved on than it was carried into effect, and I walked on foot to the Deeside home of the Queen with anything but a *decided* success.

I resolve to see the Queen,

Leaving Dundee one glorious summer morning, I determined to go to Balmoral, and lay all my grievances at the foot of the throne in person. I resolved, after reading—as I myself modestly aver I only can—such pieces of my own to Her Majesty as seemed to me most calculated to impress her and stir up her royal emotions, to put the question plainly to her whether I had deserved the treatment I had got at the hands, feet, and lungs of her Dundee subjects. But, alas, misfortune still dogged my heels.

To give my readers some little idea of my public spirit, sense of duty, and indomitable pluck, I may mention that on starting my commissariat consisted solely of half a pound of cheese and six oatcakes; while the exchequer amounted all told to one shilling and fourpence. Of course, I made no provision for a return journey, relying on the assumption that the royal sense of justice would perceive the utter incongruity of the compiler of so much sublimity grovelling in a single-roomed den; while minor stars, not fit to be named in the same breath as Shakespeare and myself, revelled in sumptuous luxuriousness.

So far as "togs" were concerned, my fears centred most completely on my boots. As I surveyed them they actually gaped at me. Fancy how they yawned after sixty miles through a dreary wilderness of heath and heather, with nothing to vary the monotony but thunder storms and waterspouts, which, first reducing my paper collar to a pulp, speedily ran down inside my garments, and obtained exit at the aforesaid cracks, the utility of which I never before comprehended.

Lovely gorges. Pic-nicers and English swells dilate on the lovely gorges you pass through on the Balmoral road. I was more concerned about the lovely gorges which should have entered into me.

Tired and hungry, I at length arrived at the gates of the castle, which were opened by one who asked me in a southern accent what the nature of my business was. I told him I had called to see the Queen in order to demand, what she was bound to grant to the very meanest of her subjects, Justice.

"What are you?" he asked.

"I am a poet," I replied.

"Your demand," he said sternly, "smacks more of the Anarchist than the poet, and your looks would pass for either—the same lantern jaws, hungry looks, long hair, and light blue eyes. I don't know quite where to place you."

"This is my work, sir," I rejoined, handing him the new twopenny edition of my poems. He looked carefully over it for fully five minutes in utter silence, smiling all the while. At length he looked squarely at me, and said, "I have you now. Have you broken loose?"

"No," I said, understanding his allusion thoroughly, "but I have broken heads in my time on less provocation."

"Oh, ho, my bold boy; I know *your* sort. I've been a keeper myself, and have put a straight jacket on a man three times as big as you."

"You English fool," I shouted, losing my temper, "do you take me for a lunatic."

"You admitted being a poet," he coolly retorted; "what's the difference? All poets are fools; hungry and ragged poets are idiots; and a poet who thinks that Her Majesty would accord him an interview is simply stark, staring mad."

"Was your own countryman, Tennyson, mad?" I asked.

He winced visibly at this, then said, "No, not he; he was long haired and long faced, to be sure; but he was a rich man, and a lord to boot. Moreover, he was bound to have written better stuff than you, or he would have been neither."

"Is that your standard of a great poet, 'rich, and a lord,'" I exclaimed in disgust. "Look here, sir, than those poems you hold in your hand (and for which you have not paid me) there is no better poetry anywhere, not even your vaunted Lord Tennyson's. He is rich and I am poor, as a man; he is poor and I am rich, as a poet."

A fool's standard of a poet.

"Let me hear one of your pieces," he said, laughing, as if I had just said something very funny.

"No, sir," I thundered, "I am no strolling mountebank, and would not recite in the open-air to the Queen herself, let alone to one who is evidently an enemy of mine."

At this the man grew quite angry, threw twopence at me, and told me to clear out, or I would be arrested.

It began to dawn on me by this time that that man might be a friend or a relation even of Tennyson's, and when he found out that I was indeed a poet he was alarmed. So I cleared out, and he shut the gate, through which, like the righteous man of old, I had not been ashamed to speak unto mine enemy.

A reception like this would have daunted any mortal of ordinary calibre, but adversity had so long followed me that I was schooled to bear rebuffs with that equanimity which distinguishes genius from the ordinary herd. Still, being hungry, penniless, and footsore, I must confess to a temptation to shake the dust from my feet in anger against the palace gates. Nay, more, I would have done so, but from the fear that the soles might have parted in the process, and

I come home like an old time friar.

compelled me to proceed on my homeward march more like a mediæval friar than a modern poet. Therefore, with a careful sigh, I turned my back on Balmoral, disgusted at my failure, and hoping, if I could only keep from coughing and sneezing, that I and the most of my garments would arrive eventually at Paton's Lane.

We got home in company, bar the paper collar, which was totally past redemption ere I reached the Spittal of Glenshee. The boots, with the aid of lemonade wires and pieces of cord, not only held out bravely, but they looked all the more picturesque, and felt all the more comfortable, for these adventitious aids, which gave them the appearance of the foot gear of a Bedouin Arab.

CHAPTER VII.

I GO TO LONDON.

> He came, he saw, but that was all,
>   The thing's beyond dispute;
> The "conquering," like the ancient Gaul,
>   Was on the other foot.—*Camberwell Sneerer.*

AFTER my return from Balmoral, I felt so downcast and fatigued that I kept the house for a whole week, during which time I had fully summed up the dismal situation. Need I recapitulate: everything had failed me, and still I was unbeaten. But if ever a man prayed fervently to get away from any place, I was that man, and that place was Dundee.

The answer to that prayer, strange to say, was brought about by a silly hoax. Heaven sent it, although the devil brought it. A letter reached me exactly a week after my return to the following effect:—

Her Majesty's Theatre,
Dundee, ———.

DEAR MR M'GONAGALL,—Being in Dundee, and on the outlook for a gentleman to play leading tragedy parts in London and the provinces, I would be pleased to have an interview with you, at twelve noon, at Stratton's, Reform Street, where you, I, and a few friends can have lunch together, and a talk over matters, which I hope will lead to business to our mutual advantage.—Yours truly,

DION BOUCICAULT.

Punctually at the time mentioned I put in an appearance, and was shown upstairs to a smoking-room, in which were seated ten or a dozen gentlemen, most of whom were known to me. At the head of the table was a good looking, elderly gentleman, who was a perfect stranger. He was introduced to me as Dion Boucicault, and he looked the part so well that I thoroughly believed I had the honour of grasping in friendship the hand of the great playwright. He said he liked my appearance and the tones of my voice; would I object to give him a specimen of my powers.

I am introduced to an imposter.

"Certainly not, Mr Boucicault, I will only be too glad," I replied, "and if you can give me an engagement in London it will take me out of the greatest difficulty I was ever in in my life. Do you know, sir, if the magistrates of Dundee knew I was to have been here they certainly would have taken steps to prevent this meeting."

"Incredible," cried the great man in astonishment. "Envy, I suppose; never mind. If I mistake not, the tables will soon be turned when you appear as leader of my company at Her Majesty's Theatre here, and receive a cake and wine banquet from these same magistrates. But, now to business; let us hear you, Mr M'Gonagall."

Thus encouraged, I gave him my own "Bannockburn," and selections from Shakespeare, Macbeth, Hamlet, and Richard the Third, until the panes in the glass roof rattled with the vigour of my declamation and the thunder of applause which followed. Boucicault was more than satisfied, and offered me £123 10s a week, bed, board, and washing, which I at once accepted.

But now an eye-opener occurred. The lunch was called in, and judge my surprise when I found it to consist of a small glass of beer and the thinnest cut ham sandwich I ever saw or thought possible to make. I have been told that a sovereign can be beaten out to cover the front of a whole block of four storey buildings; but the man who cut that ham, which lay between two emaciated slices of bread, could easily have covered an acre with one of Johnnie Wood's 16-pounders.

Imposition detected by a piece of ham.

No wonder my suspicions were aroused, even although they had not left the room, laughing like to split, and tumbling over each other as they ran down the steep wooden stair, and left me all alone with the precious lunch. After thinking the matter over, I made for the theatre, saw Mr Hodges, and had my suspicions thoroughly confirmed. Mr Boucicault had not been in Dundee for a very long time, and the letter, which I left with Mr Hodges, was not in his hand-writing.

Mr Hodges, it seems, had forwarded the letter to the great Dion, and he, like the large-hearted man he really was, sent me £5 by way of solatium, as he expressed it, to heal my wounded feelings. Need any one who knows me guess the brilliant thoughts which now assailed me. The finger of Providence was surely here this time. London! Five pounds!! Dion Boucicault!!! To London I resolved to go, and wrote to my patron Dion that I would call on him personally and thank him for his kind encouragement to a poor but meritorious poet and player, that he need not be at the trouble to meet me at Wapping, as I could call at his theatre and give him a few specimens,

I resolve to storm London.

and that I would be greatly astonished, if he was not, concluding a remarkable epistle with a sample of native poetical genius to the effect that when the Governor among the nations at the great day examined every man's record, that

> "With thy soul He will find no fault,
> My own dear Dion Boucicault."

This, I imagined, would fetch him; but we shall see.

With the aid of a few friends I got up a farewell entertainment, which came off quite unknown to the authorities in the Argyle Hall, which was crowded in every part. On this occasion I was presented with a ham, in the centre of which was inserted a big brass plate bearing the legend, "A meat offering from Dundee to M'Gonagall." Considering the state of the larder at the time, this was indeed a meet as well as a meat offering. On this occasion also a prize, consisting of a quarter stone of sausages, was offered for the best poem on "M'Gonagall."

This had been advertised for a week previous, and was decided at the meeting. The result was a tie betwixt two, which I give in full. As both authors felt offended at not getting an undivided award, the prize was handed to me, and though I would not take it upon me to assert that the poems were unapproachable, I do emphatically aver that the prize was, and had to be, tackled strategically. Here they are :—

> M'Gonagall, the silvery,
>   Before you leave these walls,
> Before you go to London town
>   To join your tragic pals.

We feel constrained to tell you,
   Before this raging crowd,
That you're a bard, and no mistake,
   Of whom Dundee is proud.

And if for two or three bob you act,
   So marvellously here;
How will you soar in Drury Lane,
   With thousands every year.

Fare thee well, thou gifted bard,
   May fortune cheer thee ever,
And send at least, when famished hard,
   A modicum of liver.

But if neglected thou should'st roam,
   No bed, however hard;
Take this farewell advice, and seek
   The nearest casual ward.

And write a letter to Dundee,
   Though you a penny lack,
And willing friends around you here
   Will pay your passage back.

And when you reach Victoria Dock,
   Let this dispel your gloom,
Though hard up here, you're better far
   Than in a London tomb.

The other one is longer, and also fairly good for an amateur, and runs thus:—

Robert Burns, in dulcet strains,
   Sweetly sang o' love and lasses;
Dundee's poet, with greater brains,
   Far the Ayrshire bard surpasses.

"Scots wha hae" is very good,
   An', dootless, answered weel its turn ;
But viewed as patriotic food,
   Could ne'er compare with "Bannockburn."

To "A' the airts the wind can blaw"
   We willingly wad boo the knee ;
But, Lord, it's no a sang ava
   Like "Broon haired lassie o' Dundee."

Byron's rhymes nae better fared
   Than his o' bonnie Doon ;
An' a' his English friends despaired
   When they saw thy "Silvery Moon."

England's bard, the gentle Will,
   England thocht wad still hold sway ;
Doon he drapt like half o' gill
   At the sough o' "Silvery Tay."

Ower a' the bards together put,
   Frae Friockheim to Japan,
He towers aloft, beyond dispute,
   Creation's greatest man.

Oh, had he lived 'mang ancient Greeks,
   He wad been crooned wi' laurels ;
Instead o' wearin' cast-off breeks,
   An' livin' on dry farls.

For shame, Dundee ! when he's a spook,
   His pearls may amend you ;
They re-cast here now, what says the book ?
   "They turn again and rend you."

Bouch, because a brig he planned;
  Oh, how I blush to write it,
Was made before the Queen to stand,
  And wi' a sword be knighted.

Oh, greater Bouch, by far than he,
  Greater far, though slighted;
A greater far than even she,
  Dubbed you, alas! be-nighted.

This entertainment, bar the animal and vegetable curiosities which were showered on me, proved a tolerable success, for, besides the ham, which was well matured, as all Mr Wood's generally were, I got twenty shillings, part of which I had to invest in astringents for self and all who partook of the lively present. Another interesting item on the programme on this occasion was a plebiscite taken to decide whether Shakespeare or myself were likely to be the more popular in London, the flattering result being a dead tie, the chairman refusing on the score of the exceeding gravity of the question to give a casting vote, further than to say that, in his opinion, Shakespeare and M'Gonagall were much alike, especially Shakespeare.

A plebiscite between Shakespeare and myself.

For this sensible utterance I now take the opportunity of publicly thanking the gentleman, and also informing him that he did well in leaning a little in favour of Shakespeare, whom I consider about the ablest and wisest man that ever lived. I do not deny that, had I lived before him, he might have been ever greater than he was, even as I am now greater, because he lived before me. Be that as it may, however, I was glad to have it in my power to tell Dion on my arrival in London of the very near squeak our mutual friend, William, had had for it.

In due time the fateful day arrived, and I presented myself at the London boat about an hour and a half before the advertised time of its departure, my only luggage consisting of a few paper collars and a supply of visiting cards, printed by a friend in Dundee on large envelopes, with the flaps cut off, something like this :—

*Signifies Lyric Inditer and Reciter.

> WM. MACGONAGALL, *L.I.A.R.*,*
> SUCCESSOR TO
> WM. SHAKESPEARE.
> POETRY PROMPTLY EXECUTED.

After waving a thousand adieus to my native land, my congregated friends, and pinching poverty, the gallant vessel steamed off, and the bard "was alone on the unconscious sea," alone to meditate on coming greatness and grandeur, now that he had immediate prospects of a helping hand from a living and successful play writer. Having nothing to disturb the calm serenity of my soul, not even the knawings of hunger, I gave full rein to my imagination, and allowed it ample scope to soar whithersoever it would. I saw in my mind's eye copies of my "Newport Railway" stuck all over the North Pole.

I give rein to my imagination.

I heard the parrots in the torrid zones of the sunny south whistling in melodious accents "The bonnie broon haired lassie." I felt the sough of the plumed pines of Kamschatska as they swayed to the low and mournful cadences of my funeral pieces; while the bird of Paradise, in heavenly hues arrayed, warbled in orange groves amid seraphic splendour my glorious "Ode to the Moon." The bul-bul, amidst the thousand glories of the primeval forest whistled in my raptured ears to the tattooed chiefs and his dusky squaw all the glorious symphonies of the great M'Gonagall.

I saw the "Bruce of Bannockburn" blot out as a recitation for ever the "Half a League" of my weaker English rival; while I myself starred the London stage, with the plaudits of press and people ringing in my ears like the roar of the sea around me.

These sights and sounds soon lulled me to sleep, to be present in dreams in a more exaggerated form;

Rocked in the cradle of the deep.

for in these dreams I imagined that the advent of the millenium was to be due mainly to the sublime literature which emanated from my fertile brain. Alternating thus between sleeping and waking visions, Wapping drew nigh, and I heard a sound of music on the shore. Thinking my patron had been at the expense of a brass band to welcome me, I asked one of the passengers, an intelligent looking man, if he could detect the tune they were playing. My thoughts were confirmed when he stated that it was "Lo he comes to Wapping," a tune I never heard of before, but thought it most appropriate; the only thing which puzzled me being why the composer had styled me Lochee, instead of Dundee, if I was the central idea in the flattering programme.

Wondering sore which was the true elucidation of the incident, we arrived and landed; but no Boucicault was there, only a German band blowing away like blazes to all and sundry "Oh why left I my hame." This, my first sell in London, was both appropriate and prophetic. But as the poet somewhere remarks—

> "'Twere long to tell, and sad to trace,
> Each step from splendour to disgrace."

From the aforesaid visions aboard ship, from the myrtle groves of Arcadia, to that beastly buggy dungeon of a common lodging-house, called the "White Horse," in Fetter Lane, surrounded by drunken blackguards, and squalor of the lowest London type; but I suppose I must go on with it, although I am anticipating. Well, then, save the booming of some big clocks, nothing striking occurred until I reached the aforesaid "bunk," and showed the landlord my card, at which the undiscerning idiot actually laughed. Smothering my indignation with the cheering thought that the laugh would soon be on my side, I engaged a bed, for which I paid sixpence in advance, and set out for the Adelphi Theatre to see my friend.

I visit Boucicault. Arrived there, I sent up my card, and the manager appeared presently, tearing it up and telling me sternly all the while that "Mr Boucicault was too busy at any time ever to see me," and before I could either remonstrate or explain he disappeared, and, as John Bunyan would say, "I saw him no more."

This was horrible, and so dreadfully different from what I fully expected, that I actually burst into tears, and departed to seek Henry Irving at the Lyceum. Again sending up my card, another managerial looking specimen appeared "more potent than the last." After looking at me from head to foot, he asked if I really thought Mr Irving would speak to me?

This terrible question was asked in such scathing and contemptuous tones that I could not resist striking my most tragic attitude and belching in my deepest thunder, "Tell Henry Irving that I consider myself a far greater man than he is, and I hope we will both live long enough for him to acknowledge it."

Screwed off at the meter in this abrupt and unceremonius manner, my spirits fell below zero, and I turned my back on those two jealous actors with mixed feelings of pity and indignation, and sought the solitude of my chamber at the "White Horse." Did I say solitude? Well, I thought I was alone till I ventured between the sheets, and then I was painfully undeceived. The only thing I was thankful for was that they were not all of one mind, as Charles Lamb puts it, or they might have pulled me on to the floor. What a restless night I did have, and yet it had its ludicrous aspect after all. One enormous fellow, shaped somewhat like a flounder, had fallen overboard into a vessel he had not calculated on, and swimming on to a raft, consisting of a spent lucifer match, he kept circling round and round in this miniature china sea, walloping his arms sailor-like, and singing lustily "A life on the ocean wave."

The singing bug.

The situation had a serious bearing as well, inasmuch as that night's experience entirely changed my political views. Before this I was a Radical, holding, as one of the cardinal points of my political creed, that tenants should be allowed to destroy their own game. I am now a Tory in this respect, and strongly believe in the exclusive right and bounden duty of the landlord to decimate his own vermin, and leave his tenants unmolested. This explanation I heartily commend to Mr Jenkins as quite as true, less prolix, and more practical than his mundane evolution theory. The metamorphosis can be explained in far fewer words than he uses. It was a big bug in Belfast which converted him. It was a big bug in Babylon that changed me.

After passing a miserable night I arose, cooked my own breakfast, and set out to purchase writing materials, and immediately thereafter indited two peppery epistles, one to Irving and the other to Boucicault, telling them plainly my mission in London, my expectations of assistance from them, and the disappointing result; asking them plainly whether or not it was by their direction that their subordinates had so snubbed me, and requesting a reply in due course to the "White Horse." But no answer ever came.

I felt furious, but gradually cooled down in the exact ratio of the diminishing of my funds. Beef, you know, from its inflammatory nature, is well **The inflammatory** calculated to keep up red hot choler; but **nature of beef.** an occasional red herring, with dry bread and terribly wet, weak tea at most irregular intervals, takes the high falutin out of a fellow wonderfully. Well then, it was after a sustained regimen of this sort that I even got so tame as to make allowances for the extraordinary conduct of those two men.

They were already at the top of the tree, I argued, and could rise no higher, even with my assistance; while, on the other hand, the chances were that if the public saw and appreciated me, I might have gone up and forced them to come down. Be this as it may, I never got the chance, or I would not now be under the necessity of covering so much paper for a "bob."

They know it, and I know it, and it is not my fault now if the whole world does not know it. It was a strong combination, perhaps the strongest which could have been arrayed against me; but it did not break me. At the present moment, sufficient funds provided, I am as willing as ever to try my fortune again in London.

Meantime, however, I was glad, having nothing to feed the fishes with, to commit myself once more to the briny, and leave the inhospitable hulk of a town, en route for Dundee, a poorer, a hungrier, but not a less hopeful man.

CHAPTER VIII.

I GO TO NEW YORK.

> I love New York, for it made me
>   Love my own land the better;
> For this I certainly will be
>   Its everlasting debtor.—"*The Emigrant's Return.*"

ON my return from London I was strongly urged by the members of my own household to desert the muses, as I did not seem to be appreciated anywhere, my wife telling me that I might take it as a sign that the genius had possibly made a mistake, and brought the commission to the wrong door.

"Avaunt!" I cried, "and tempt me not; ye all speak about the genius as if she were a half drunk postman who mixes up his deliveries. I will never desert the post she placed me at, until she appears again and tells me to do so. Know once for all that I am irrepressible."

And I beg here and now to repeat to the whole world that, though I have been discouraged and crushed a thousand times, I have always risen again triumphant, and this is my manifesto to all whom it may concern: "I have nailed the colours of my poetical genius to the mast of my own appreciation, and twenty thousand demons in the shape of adverse critics cannot rend them asunder."

I say, like Martin Luther, on some of his friends trying to dissuade him from going in for a "diet of worms, " If every tile on every housetop was a devil, I must go on." Dundee has failed me, London has turned out a frost ; but, thank God, the world is wide, and that there are other and better places than either. I am told if I only could get to America I would soon make a fortune ; that on **Visions of** the streets of New York, instead of a paltry **dollars.** penny given grudgingly for a copy of my poems, I would get a dollar, and the buyer would feel himself the obliged party. Ah, me! What would it be to be there? At length a bright idea struck me, and no sooner did it do so than I put the wisely conceived plan into execution.

I got a pass book, setting forth on the first page that I wished to go to America, and that those willing to assist me in this project would have the opportunity of putting down their names as subscribers. I was successful beyond my most sanguine expectations, and felt sure that the tide had turned at last. Friend and foe alike contributed : the former, I afterwards learned, to oblige me ; and the latter to get rid of what they deemed a nuisance. At the time I was blind enough not to perceive this, although my suspicions ought to have been aroused from the fact that two of the magistrates subscribed five shillings each.

It was Mr Lamb, of Lamb's Hotel, who pointed this out to me, when I had raised sufficient money, and went to bid him good-bye. "Mr M'Gonagall," he said, "this money, I am sure, has been given you largely by pretended friends, who want you to lose yourself in America ; but we will thwart their fell purpose yet. I gave ten shillings to help you off, but if ever you wish to come back I will send you your passage money." So saying, we shook hands and parted, I little dreaming how soon I would have to avail myself of his magnanimous offer.

Full of hope, fuller than ever, I took train to Glasgow, and was soon on board the good ship "Circassian," in which I had secured a steerage passage.

An unremunerated entertainment. The voyage was rough, but otherwise uneventful. On one occasion I was asked into the second cabin to give an entertainment. There was a collection taken, which I expected to receive; but the steward intervened with the announcement that no collection could be taken on board that ship except for the lifeboat fund, and so I was done out of it, and declined all further invitations of this nature during the voyage.

On arrival at Castle Gardens, I had to declare myself a labourer. If I had said I was a poet they would have turned me back. The authorities then asked me if I had any money. I said I had, and was going to friends; taking out all I had I asked them with as careless an air as I could assume to give me American money for eight shillings to meet immediate requirements.

I am sorry now I did not tell them the whole truth; that I was a poet, and that all I had in the world was eight shillings. They would then have refused to allow me to proceed farther, have sent me back, and saved me a lot of misery and cruel disillusionment.

Having the address of an old acquaintance and admirer in Dundee, I took a car there, was warmly welcomed, and partook of a hearty tea, in return for which I imparted all the latest gossip from Juteopolis. Having arranged to take up my abode with my newly found friends, who were people of the better sort, we spent the evening for the most part in arranging my plan of campaign. I had with me a plentiful supply of poems and twopenny editions of my works, which I expected to clear off speedily at half a dollar and a dollar respectively. These, however, we arranged to leave alone meantime, the conclave deciding that it would be better for me to try the music halls and theatres first for a permanent engagement. Armed, therefore, with a specimen of each of my own productions, and brimful of anticipation, I started forth, not like Christopher Columbus, merely to discover America, but more important still, to allow America to discover me.

Difference between Columbus and me.

Sauntering leisurely along in order to assimilate myself to my new surroundings, I at length reached a palatial looking building at the corner of Broadway and some other street—which I was correct in taking for a theatre. I entered its portals, crossed the floor of the hallway, and rung an electric bell at the side of a window, on which was inscribed "Enquiry Office." In a moment the window was opened, and a gentleman in a gold laced hat and gilt buttons asked me my business.

"I want to see the manager," I said.

"Have you a card?" he inquired.

I produced one of those I had used in London. Like all the Londoners who were privileged to receive one, he immediately commenced to laugh. I was getting sick of this, and resolved to show no more of them, the affixed initials being evidently taken too literally, and altogether misapprehended. "Friend," I said as severely as I could, "you are not laughing so much at my card as at your own ignorance. Take it to the manager at once."

With another burst of hilarity he disappeared, came back in a minute, and told me to follow him. Up stairs he went, I after him, till we reached a handsome picture-pannelled door, which he opened, showed me in with a bow, withdrew, and left me standing in the most gorgeous apartment I ever saw. In the centre of this perfect room, seated at a desk, was a man about my own age, with a red face and a white moustache and goatee. Speaking with a strong nasal twang, and pointing with his finger to a chair beside me, he said: "So, so! You air a pro-fessional liar? Sit down."

A Yankee speaks.

"Sir," I said, "you have made a mistake; I am no liar. The L.I.A.R. at my name stands for Lyric Inditer and Reciter."

"Ah!" he said, "if I had known that I would not have troubled you. I am not interested in lyrics, good, bad, or indifferent; and loonatics are common enough here, not to be very interesting. But I do dote on a powerful liar with a big L; they're all the rage on this side. I perceive you air a Britisher."

"I am, sir; and I am sorry to hear that liars are such favourites in New York."

"There's nothing else, in any line, of any use here. Are you an actor?" he inquired.

"I am a poet and tragedian from Dundee, in Scotland, seeking an engagement," I answered. "Of course," I continued, "if you engage me as an actor I can only speak the lines set down for me, and cannot, therefore, vouch for their veracity. But in all my poems and songs the name

'M'Gonagall' stamped on them is a guarantee of purity and truth."

"Wall, old man, look here," he said, "I reckon you might be a tragedian without being much of a stranger to the truth, especially if you managed to steer clear of the plays of that effete old liar of yours you call Shakespeare. But if you stick no stretches in your poetry it would taste as tame as porridge without oatmeal."

In wrath, which I could only partially conceal, I pulled out my Newport Railway poem—the most moral of the batch—and, spreading it out before him, defied him to find the slightest shadow of a lie in it from Alpha to Omega.

Looking at it for two or three minutes, then holding his sides with his hands, he roared with laughter till his red face grew purple.

"Right you air," he cried, as soon as he could articulate. "I apologise, Mr. . For this is indeed the porridge without the oatmeal, or the salt either, by the great Jehoshaphat !! By heaven, this is the very essence of fun ! Mark Twain, my boy, look to your laurels !! This old buck presses you vurry, vurry hard !!" "You a tragedian." he continued betwixt the paroxisms. "Why, man alive, you are the very lowest low comedy, side-splitting funniosity, on the face of the earth."

His laughter irritated me tremendously. "Sir," I said, boiling with righteous indignation, "you have the audacity to call Shakespeare a liar ; and you compare my poems to porridge. I tell you to your face, you are a mendacious liar, a blackguard, a traducer, and a mocker at morality. I would not take an engagement from you at £1000 a week."

"Splendid! Capital! Bravo!" he roared, as I made for the door. "By thunder, that man will kill me."

"Amen," I replied, as I banged his painted panels, and left the premises.

Shocked and disgusted, but carrying my head erect, as best beseemed one who had scored heavily in the interests of morality, I made for another place of entertainment not far off. I sent no card on this or any subsequent occasion, having now become thoroughly convinced that these cards were intended by the man who printed them for me as a regular "cod," to make people laugh at me. Walking, therefore, right into the vestibule, I saw a man, tall, thin, and sallow, with firmly compressed lips, and wearing a frock coat and silk hat. I accosted him, and asked if I could see the "boss." "You do see him," he drawled. I lifted my hat and said, "Sir, you see before you a tragedian in poor circumstances, anxious to have an opportunity of appearing before an American audience."

I discard cards.

"Don't try it, my good man," he answered, piercing me with his eagle eye. "Take my advice, and get over the water again as soon as you can, as the prejudice is so great on this side against British actors that I would to a certainty get my show wrecked right away if any of them appeared on my stage. And I feel certain," he added with a mocking smile, "that you are the last man to contemplate such a catastrophe with equanimity."

"I certainly am, sir. But what am I to do; I have no money," I replied.

"That's bad," he said; "but I can't help you in any way. Get your friends on the other side to scrape up the price of your passage. You will never manage to do it yourself in New York. Go straight home, and write to Andrew Carnegie for an organ. They tell me he gives them away for nothing."

"Not to private individuals, sir; only to churches," I anwered. "Mr Carnegie is a good man and benevolent; is very willing to help his countrymen; but, in my opinion, he goes a somewhat strange way about it. We in Scotland have a song about a piper who had a cow, and no food to give her, so he took his pipes and played a tune to the poor famished beast, entitled 'Corn rigs are bonnie.' There are thousands in Scotland at this moment good, honest, virtuous men and women, who, with their children, are at the point of starvation through no fault of their own. Mr Carnegie's organs will do as much good to them as the piper's tune did to the cow, or as your advice will do to me. Good morning, sir."

<small>Music for the hungry.</small>

You may wonder why I cut this interview so short. I will tell you. I knew intuitively from the expression of his face that he was a hard, greedy man. I knew that he lied when he told me that there was a prejudice against British artistes, as Henry Irving, Dion Boucicault, and all the other stars of our country were always rapturously received in America; and I know also that he had formed a very poor opinion of my abilities as an actor, when he suggested I should take to organ grinding for a livelihood. Such is my Sherlock Holmes-like power of penetration that I felt that no succour of any kind was to be expected from this quarter. So I went home to dinner, and related my adventures.

It was decided that I should tackle the man on the street with my poems next day. The place chosen was a back road in the vicinity of "The Bowery." The first man I interviewed had a sad expression on his somewhat comely face. I held out my "Spittal of Glenshee" poem to him. He looked at it solemnly, shook his head, and said "Nein, nein."

I thought he wanted nine copies, and felt quite elated. I counted them out, and handed them to him, saying "Four dollars, please;" but he brushed them aside with the same "Nein, nein."

I then commenced to read the poem to him, watching his face all the time. Ever and anon as I proceeded his expression grew more and more stolid and impassive; not a smile, not a single gleam of intelligence illumined his weather-beaten face. I might as well have been reading a chapter to a horse for all the impression I was making. The quadruped would possibly have interpolated in his own way with the frequency of the man's "Nein, neins;" but the net results, so far as it and I were concerned, would have been precisely the same, as I now experienced. At length a bystander, who had been attracted to the spot, informed me that he was a German emigrant newly landed, on which I desisted, and addressing my informant, said "Will you buy a poem?"

Reading a chapter to a horse.

"No, sir, I would not take one for nothing," he replied.

"It is a splendid work I assure you," I urged. "It is 'The Spittal of Glenshee,' and only half a dollar."

He snorted indignantly, "Go on; who are you trying to get at? I would not give you half a cent for all the spittals in New York."

I expect the ignorant fellow thought I referred to expectorations, not knowing the difference, nor at all anxious to learn, for he made off with his nose in the air. The next I ventured to accost was evidently a red hot Republican, for he asked me "if I was not ashamed to parade the Royal Arms of England through the streets of a free country."

"No, sir," I said, "I am a loyal subject of the Queen of Britain, and will stick to my colours."

"Take my advice, old man," he said not unkindly, "don't risk your life at this game, or more than one stick may stick your vaunted colours of red, white, and blue all over your carcase. The symbols of tyranny will not go down here," he continued earnestly, "unless to be trampled in the gutter. If your poems are good and anti-monarchal, tear off the Royal Arms and they'll maybe fetch a cent a piece; otherwise, if you escape lynching by the mob, it will only be to fall into the hands of the police on a charge of inciting to riot. Of course, you can please yourself, boss, it's nothing to me; but my straight advice to you is to show no more of them in this country. I like to see a plucky man, but I reckon it's going a bit too strong to risk your life for a cent or two."

"A what?" I cried. "My price for each poem is half a dollar."

"Half a dollar!" he shouted. "Are you mad; if you're not, I'll lay a bet you don't sell a single copy between now and the day of judgment," and he passed on without exhibiting the slightest curiosity as to the nature of their contents.

In stress and storm.

On turning to go home it began to snow very heavily, so that by the time I reached my attic I presented the appearance of a regular Father Christmas. I did not sleep that night, the cold was so intense; this and the terror I was in owing to the things that Republican had told me kept me very wide awake; and to crown all, I was called at six o'clock next morning to break sticks and sweep away the snow. Oh, heavens, to think of it! A duly ordained poet a hewer of wood and a shoveller of snow.

Every day for a fortnight I tramped the length and breadth of New York seeking anything to do, but no one would listen to me or give me a single red cent. I do not understand the American people at all. My poems did not interest them in the slightest. Any one I accosted simply passed on without a word, good or bad. My isolation was painfully complete. I was not sneered at or despised; I was not made the victim of horse play. I almost wished I had been; anything in the world rather than to be ignored. I was absolutely helpless and useless, fighting the wind and beating my hands against unresisting air. Some treated me as a lunatic, others as a mendicant, but nobody ever dreamed of discussing the point. Oh, the utter desolation of it.

I used to envy the poet Homer his exemption from the striking attentions which had fallen so plentifully to my lot. I now recant that envy, and pity the poor old soul from the bottom of a fellow-feeling heart, for I have now come to the conclusion that any sort of attentions are preferable to this cold American indifference,

In Dundee I was dead value for something like a "bob a bruise." Now I actually felt that I would gladly have had a few of them at a considerably reduced figure.

Do you wonder then that all my energies were now directed to getting back to Dundee as fast as possible? The first step was to write to Mr A. C. Lamb asking him, for God's sake, to redeem the captivity of his humble servant according to promise. This I did, posted it, and waited. In due course I called at the shipping office of the Anchor Line, to which address I had instructed Mr Lamb to reply. I asked Mr Stewart, the manager, if there was any letter for me.

"Oh, yes; it's all right," was the cheering answer. "I had a cable from Mr Lamb to give you a second cabin passage back and six pounds.

This I got half in American money and half in British, along with my ticket for the same vessel (the "Circassian") as I had come out in. I nearly fainted with joy, a most unusual predicament for me.

I compose on the briny.

In due time I arrived in Dundee, having occupied my time during the passage to Glasgow in writing a poem of fifteen stanzas, which will live, if for nothing else than the faithful picture it gives of New York and my feelings at leaving it. It is too long to insert here, but I give you the four concluding stanzas :—

And there are also ten thousand rum sellers there,
Oh, wonderful to think of, I do declare;
To accommodate the people of New York therein,
And to encourage them to commit all sorts of sin.

And on the Sabbath day ye will see many a man
Going for beer with a big tin can,
And seems proud to be seen carrying home the beer,
To treat his neighbours and his family dear.

Then at night numbers of people dance and sing,
Making the walls of their homes to ring
With their songs and dancing on Sabbath night;
Which I witnessed with disgust, and fled from the sight.

And with regard to New York and the sights I did see,
Believe me, I never saw such sights in Dundee;
And the morning I sailed from the city of New York,
My heart it felt as light as a cork.

This, my dear friends in its entirety, is one of the finest poems in the English language.

CHAPTER IX.

I Take Glasgow by Storm.

"Where hath Scotland found her glory?"
   Whence her mighty enterprise?
   Let St Mungo tell the story,
   For in her the answer lies.—"*Old Song.*"

ON landing at Glasgow, I had some time to wait for a train to Dundee. This gave me a long wished for opportunity of seeing the sights of St. Mungo, which are really much better worth a visit than I had imagined. When I began to write uninspired poetry, as you are aware, I included Glasgow in the scope of my themes, a proof that my spirit sometimes wandered west; but when I wrote that "the prettiest river that ever I saw was Glasgow on the Clyde," it was merely a poet's licence, and a proof of my unlimited imagination—a faculty which the vulgar construe vulgarly.

For, save for my visit to America, my bodily perigrinations had hitherto been exclusively confined to the east of Scotland, the glories of which had so filled my mind to the exclusion of all others, that I thought I had seen and heard all that was worth seeing and hearing, at least in the land of my birth.

I was like the trout who lived in a three-acre pond—very difficult to persuade that there was anything of any consequence outside of my severely proscribed limits.

America had opened my eyes in one way—it showed me that there were larger ponds than the one I grew up in, but infested with pike, who monopolised all the food, in which I myself was catalogued as one of the choicest morsels.

In Glasgow—to drop metaphor—I found a live and let live spirit, a feeling of reverence for the muses, which was carried to a very pleasant excess in their treatment of me as the embodiment of poetry. It is to hug a miserable delusion to believe that the gentlemen live in Edinburgh and the parvenues in Glasgow. This idea, owing to my experience, is now completely exploded. I must confess, however, that my conception of Glasgow before this visit was founded and fostered through the envy-begotten ideas of Edinburgh, to the effect that the sole aim and object of its inhabitants was to amass money.

I dispel a prevailing idea.

The merchant princes of St. Mungo—and I speak now from practical experience and unbounded powers of observation—are cultured gentlemen in the highest sense of the term, which simply means a due consideration for the feelings of others, a commodity they could export to the east with as little loss to themselves and as much advantage to the importers, as they do everything else which is for the benefit of mankind generally.

How strange it seems that a man of my forethought and discernment should always run up against such marvellous surprises. I feared and trembled to go to Perth; the same feeling pervaded me on taking my journey to Inverness. In both cases I was agreeably disappointed; but, as Oliver Cromwell said about the battle of Dunbar, Glasgow was "my crowning mercy." It all happened in this wise.

Amongst the many places of interest I visited was the world-famed and palatial warehouse of Mann, Byars, & Co., in whose employ was an old Dundee friend and admirer. He introduced me to the heads of the various departments, and

Merchant Princes struck with me. they were so struck with my appearance and general attainments as to resolve there and then to get up a select entertainment for me on the following evening.

They sent round the hat amongst themselves, and collected as much as kept me in comfort for the night, and something over.

The place selected was in Glassford Street, and when I appeared on the scene next evening at eight o'clock the hall was filled with the *elite* of the city. The chairman, who was introduced to me, was a Baronet and an M.P., whose name I forget. He was a powerful man, whose corporeal proportions were conceived on a generous scale. He commenced by reading letters of apology from the Lord Provost and other magnates of the city. The Russian Ambassador, Count Kutiswartzoff, a distinguished man of letters and a great poet in his own country, also sent an apology, expressed in Russian, to say how sorry he was not to have seen and heard me, or possibly to have been allowed to touch the hem of my garment, in order to carry the emanating virtue to Kamskatka, a place of sin and degredation, to which he was bound on the morrow, and to whence its efficacy might have been transmitted through his unworthy medium.

"Tell Mr M'Gonagall from me," he added, "to persevere in his great and holy mission, because nothing but the emanations from great poets will conduce to the healing of the nations and hasten the millennium. My friend, Baron Ballyrot, of the German Embassy, has expressed a strong desire to be present at your interesting levee, and though he unfortunately knows no English, yet being the greatest pantomimic and thought reader in the universe, he will be able to report the proceedings to me with an accuracy which is simply marvellous. To him, therefore, I commend you. Kindly let him have a seat on the platform."

This letter was handed to me, and then shown round the company. I have it still, but as it is written in tea box characters, I am sorry I cannot reproduce it here.

The chairman's address was a flattering appreciation of my powers as a poet and my modesty as a man. He told the audience in terms more eloquent than I can convey that there, as I sat in the garb of old Gaul, I was a sight that the very blind would rejoice to see, the greatest Scottish poet of all time, and the unique product of a century.

When the chairman sat down, a gentleman at the back of the hall, after thanking me for shedding the light of my countenance amongst them, stated that the letter of apology from the Russian Ambassador had suggested an idea. "It is all very well, he continued, "for the chairman and gentlemen on the platform to be able to touch the hem of the poet's garments, and revel in what the distinguished Count so happily characterised as 'the poetical emanation;' but," he added, "as those in the back of the hall were quite as desirous of indulging in the moral cleansing inhalation, he suggested that the poet be requested to hand round his bonnet."

An impressive ceremony. To this I readily agreed, and it was impressive to witness with what reverence they passed it carefully from one to another. Presently a shout arose, "We want more; send round his coat." To this I also agreed, though with great reluctance, as my nether garments had been last laundried at New York. Soon again, however, came the demand in strident tones from all parts of the house, "More, more; we feel better already. Send round your vest." After some persuasion from the chairman and sundry quick nods of assent from the Baron, I at length complied, and was at once complimented by the former on being a perfect presentiment of the "Dugal Cratur," which he explained was the most popular stage character in Glasgow.

This molified me somewhat, though the position struck me as being a little grotesque, considering my status as a poet and an honoured guest. After shivering till the vest went round, to my inexpressible surprise and horror, the house rose again "en masse," and shouted vociferously "The kilt, the kilt; send round the poet's kilt."

This roused me at once to prompt action, and springing to my feet, I paused for a brief space until the cries had somewhat subsided, and then in the well-known stentorian tones in which I have electrified thousands in the *role* of Macbeth, I arrested attention by that glorious outburst, "I dare all that may become a man, who does more is none." Gentlemen, I appeared before you as a poet and tragedian. At your earnest request I then assumed the character of a Highland ghillie; but I most emphatically draw the line at playing Adam before the fall in a chillier climate than Eden." At which the Baron shouted "Bravo! bravissimo! and clapped his hands, which emitted sounds like pistol shots. Truly a rare judge of histrionic ability is the Baron!

Seeing I was incensed, and backed up by the Teuton, they cheered me to the echo, and one of the audience leaped on to the platform, and facing me in the chair which I had resumed, bowed profoundly to me, and began to sing a long song with a longer refrain about a miner's daughter named

Clementine, who met a watery grave through the inordinate length of her feet. But the music and the rhythm were so sweet, melodious, and haunting that I, like King Saul under the influence of David's harp, felt instantly soothed, and began to keep time with my feet to its melodious cadences. In fact, if I had only had my clothes on I would have been perfectly happy.

At length, so pathetic was the story, so entrancing the refrain, that the entire audience, first bowing reverentially towards me, took up the theme lustily, and repeated the fascinating strain over and over again, until six or eight of them, unable to contain themselves any longer, joined the solo singer on the platform, where they clasped hands and jingo-ringed round my chair, singing louder and louder, until all traces of righteous wrath were completely exorcised, and I joined heartily in bemoaning the luckless fate of the charming Clementine.

> She drove her ducklings to the water
> Every morning just at nine;
> But her feet caught in a slipper,
> And she plunged into the brine.
>
> O, my darling! O, my darling!
> O, my darling, Clementine!
> Thou art lost, and gone for ever,
> Dreadful, sorry, Clementine.

An opportunity for a great joint effort missed.

I would I knew the author. What a collaboration he and I could make. But whether I ever meet him in the flesh or not, these words of his will haunt my soul and ring in my ears till my dying day; and from henceforth that pathetic and swinging dance with its weird-like melody will ever be associated in my mind with the witches' cauldron in Macbeth, only, instead of gruesome curiosities flung into it by "black and midnight hags," there would be the jingle of coins unstintedly rattled into the sacred circle by a crowd of well-dressed, high-souled merchant princes of Glasgow.

For the first time in my life the usual order of things was completely reversed. I was the entertained, and my audience the entertainers. It was, as I said, a unique experience, and yet I felt not the slightest desire for it to be otherwise, and between laughter and tears could have sat and sung the whole night through. But the chairman courteously reminded me that the company was impatient for pabulum of a more soul-satisfying nature, and would now hear the gospel according to M'Gonagall at my earliest convenience. This I at once proceeded to impart in such a feast of reason and a flow of soul, partly from my own works and partly from Shakespeare, that never in the annals of this or any other city was such a rational and instructive evening spent.

Even the big Baron nodded his head again in evident approval, and so well pleased was the entire company that the chairman asked if I would have anything on the following night, a question which elicited the remark from me that I could scarcely have less on any night than I had at the moment, a witticism which, amid roars of laughter, brought me the missing "togs" at once.

Whether that vast and aristocratic gathering felt better for my emanations or not, I most assuredly felt better of their's; and the sum of £4 15s., added to the balance of Mr A. C. Lamb's superb donation, enabled me with a light heart and a heavy purse, accompanied by neither wounds, bruises, or insults, to chronicle a record event in my career and a chapter virtually free from lamentations.

In honour of so unique an event, I threw my whole soul into the composition of a poem on my impressions of Glasgow, which I append with the simple remark that if the reader gets no more for his shilling than this and the cover of the book, it would save him a lot of reading, and give him the best value to be had on earth for the money.

O, beautiful city of Glasgow, which stands on the river Clyde,
How happy should the people be which in ye reside;
Because it is the most enterprising city of the present day,
Whatever anybody else may say.

The ships which lie at the Broomilaw are most beautiful to see,
They are bigger and better than any in Dundee;
Likewise the municipal buildings, most gorgeous to be seen,
Near to Ingram Street, and not far from Glasgow Green.

Then the warehouses are filled from the floor to the topmost
With goods, which brings Glasgow money and glory; [storey
And the men who own them are most liberal, I do declare,
Because I got money from them when there.

O, wonderful city of Glasgow, with your triple expansion
        engines,
At the making of which your workmen get many singeins;
Also the deepening of the Clyde, most marvellous to behold,
Which cost much money, be it told.

Then there is a grand picture gallery,
Which the keepers thereof are paid a very large salary;
Therefore, citizens of Glasgow, do not fret or worry,
For there is nothing like it in all Edinburgh.

And the happiest night I ever spent,
Was in Glasgow, where I got as much as pay my rent
From your merchant princes most fine,
Who likewise sang a song to me called Clementine;

Which was most beautiful to hear, also a dance
Round and round, all singing at once;
And the treatment I got in Glasgow, I must confess,
Was better even than Inverness.

Oh, beautiful city of Glasgow, I must conclude my lay,
By calling thee the greatest city of the present day;
For your treatment of me was by no means curlish,
Therefore I say, "Let Glasgow flourish."

You will observe that in this beautiful and exhaustive, descriptive poem I have omitted all reference to the stripping episode, because the poem, which is built to last longer than the prose on which it is set, will be read centuries after the autobiography has been consigned to forgetfulness.

CHAPTER X.

Farewell for ever to Dundee.

Hope never tires, but mounts on eagle's wings ;
Kings it makes gods, and meaner creatures kings.—Shakespeare.

ON my return to Dundee I was hopeful that my metropolitan, transatlantic, and Glasgow experience would mitigate the rigours of my condition considerably. This hope was strengthened by all sorts and conditions of men, who used to mock and maltreat me, hailing me civilly on the street, and asking me kindly all about London, Glasgow, and New York, without the slightest symptom of "codding" or the most minute attempt at personal damage.

Change of attitude towards me.

I was afraid, however, to brave the wrath of the magistrates by taking a hall for another entertainment, at least until I could ascertain whether or not their unreasonable rancour had in any way abated. Moreover, thanks to Mr Lamb and the Glasgow merchants, I was still in funds, and having a fairly high old time of it.

In the evenings, at Paton's Lane, like a second Othello, I would sit and discourse to a select coterie of admirers on my "hairbreadth escapes by flood and field," and they good, kind-hearted souls, "loved me for the dangers I had passed;" while my own heart warmed anew at their sympathy and the fervent expressions of their full belief that the dangers *were* past.

Were they? But I must not anticipate farther than by saying that the best stocked larder will soon become an empty press unless it be replenished. All too soon this became the condition of things with me, and the time at length arrived—not when the wife placed a pair of spurs on my porridge plate, after the manner of the old border raiders, but its modern equivalent in quite as understandable a fashion.

My cupboard again empty.

"Willie," cried my spouse gently but firmly, "It's a pity; but I doot you'll hae to face anither mob o' thae Dundee devils, an' that michty sune tae, or we'll hae naething to eat."

"My good woman," I replied with dignity, "I think you are labouring under a misapprehension as regards the probable treatment I will receive in the event of my getting up an entertainment."

"Maybe aye, an' maybe no," she said. "I hinna muckle faith in them mysel'; an' if ye come scaithless hame frae anither of thae entertainments, as ye ca' them, it 'll be the first time ye ever did it in a' yer life. Am no carin' sae muckle for their 'shute' or eggs, or oranges, if the ill-gated brutes wadna pap bricks and buits at ye; the ither things wid dicht aff some wy or ither. But," she continued, "if we canna get meat athoot them, there's no sae muckle hairm dune; but thae buits an' things micht mittle ye for life, or kill ye a'thegether. Man, Willie, a lion tamer's job is no half sae dangerous as yours. They've guid pey, an' they get mauled only aince in a lifetime. If you had got what you've gotten a' at ae time thir wid a been michty little o' ye left this day. It's the instalment system that's saved you, Willie; there's nae mistak' aboot that."

This was the longest speech I ever heard her deliver, and I would have been wroth at her for the lamentable lack of faith which she exhibited, had I not known from painful experience that she had good grounds for putting the devil-and-deep-sea dilemma as strongly as she had done.

Moreover, her fault, if fault it was, was temperamental, inasmuch as she lacked entirely what I have a superabundance of—the hope which believeth all things; so I calmly remarked, "If I could be sure the authorities would not object I would try it again, for I have reason to believe the people themselves are beginning to recognise my abilities at last."

"Weel, weel," she said; "buits or nae buits, you'll juist hae to risk it, for we canna stairve."

Seeing that it was useless to argue any more, I crystalised into action, and went at once to consult some of my friends. They were all of my opinion that the people were to be trusted; but that if an entertainment was got up, it would be as well to keep the knowledge of it from the powers that be.

It was ultimately suggested and carried *nem con*, that the Thistle Hall in Union Street should be taken, and the names of three or four singing friends of mine put on the bills for songs, the programme to be

I again risk acting in Dundee.

eked out with pieces "by an eminent tragedian," who did not wish his name to appear. Tickets at sixpence and one shilling each were printed, the disposers of them whispering to the purchasers, under seal of silence, the identity of the eminent tragedian.

Between the time of leasing the hall and the single night of its occupany I could neither eat nor sleep, for I felt by intuition that a full realisation of my long deferred programme had at last entered its initial stage, and that Paton's Lane and Avon would henceforth divide histrionic natal honours in equal proportions. My wife, too, poor woman, was exceedingly anxious that the result would be the maximum of coin for the minimum of disfigurement. The hour came at last, and the man; but alas!

The place was seated for over a thousand, but the programme commenced with only about three score of an audience all told; but, by jingo, the lung power of that sixty was something to remember, aided and abetted, as it was, with penny trumpets. In fact, nothing in this world could compare in extent with the noise they made, save and except the tobacco smoke they emitted in the intervals between their trumpet performances. Not a vestige of a sound could be heard all night, except a wail of mortal agony from myself on proceeding to the ante-room, to find all my togs swimming in six inches of water, and the man at the door away with the coin. As the Editor of "The Lochee Lubricator," a bit of a rhymster in his way, tolerably fairly puts it—

Fearful termination to an entertainment.

Not a verse we heard, not a single line,
   Though we strained our ears eager to catch it;
But we knew from his shapes that his muse was divine,
   And few were the bards that could match it.

They drowned him completely on that awful night,
   These rogues with their trumpets and smoke;
They cared not a fig for the brave Bruce's fight,
   And took Richard the Third for a joke.

No useless trouser encircled his groin,
   But in bonnet and tights we found him ;
And he stood like a modest tobaaconist's sign,
   With his tartan curtain around him.

Few, few, were the shillings that sat in that hall,
   And the tanners, I ween, were right rare ;
But we wondered no longer at Jericho's fall,
   And we wished all the trumpets were there.

Ah, little he thought as he glared at the rogues,
   The words of his masterpiece quoting,
That the whole of his garments and best pair of brogues
   That moment in water were floating.

Lightly they'll talk of the bard of the Tay,
   And say oh how doubly we drowned him ;
But little he'll reck if their money they pay,
   Though with trumpets they nightly surround him.

Not half of his heavy task was done,
   And the bard had no thought of retiring,
When the voice was heard of his sailor son
   For his parent loudly inquiring.

Profanely and quickly the story he told
   Of the wreck of his hat, coat, and vest ;
The side room was flooded, the bard was twice sold,
   For the man at the door was *non est*.

Slowly and sadly we led him down
   From the scene of this pitiful story ;
Dejected and sad, in his pouch not a brown,
   And we left him alone, minus glory.

As I before remarked, this describes pretty fairly the melancholy and wholly unlooked for state of affairs. God help me, I was of all men the most miserable on that bitter, beastly night. Wet and coinless, deep in debt for the hall, and the whole thing a miserable fiasco, my wife's greeting as I entered the house, "I telt you, Willie," fairly collapsed me.

I again appear at Lochee.

Goodness knows how I could have wrestled through if Michael Kinchley had not got up a levee at the Weavers' Hall, Lochee, I receiving one guinea in advance. Unlike the entertainment in the Thistle Hall, this resulted in a bumper house. I must frankly confess that, although a considerable number of my supporters were present to defend me from abuse, I approached the hall with fear and trembling. Hope seemed to forsake me, and I had a strong presentiment of an approaching donnybrook, and for once I was not mistaken.

If Dundee was bad, to what can I compare Lochee? They actually baked gingerbread on my face, one diabolical imp springing on to the platform and spreading about a pound of treacle all over my classical face ere the hand of man could prevent him. This converted me right off into a passable Othello, and was immediately followed from all parts of the house by well directed missiles in the shape of thin paper bags filled with flour, which burst like bombshells where they struck, turning poor bewildered Othello into Hamlet's father's ghost. A few eggs were added, the gingerbread completed, and my utter discomfiture accomplished, for I must say that I lost my temper most completely on this occasion, and struck out blindly with my stick all round, and amid falling forms and shouts of murder had to be run incontinently into the ante-room by two stalwart policemen, leaving the brutal mob of Low-he men clamouring at the door like the ruffians of Sodom for Lot's visitors. After an angry caution from the policemen, and a solemn promise cheerfully given never again to appear in Lochee, I was escorted home wonderfully sound in wind and limb.

And now I have to record my last public appearance in Dundee, having in consequence of another intimation resolved to take up my residence in the fair city of Perth. This fact coming to the ears of a few fiends, my presence was requested at a farewell levee in the Lorne Bar in Bank Street to receive a silvery collection and my portrait in oil. I hied there at the time appointed, and full of hope and "bridies," awaited the presentation. Fancy my utter disgust when, instead of a life-size oil painting by Millais, a pencil sketch the size of an ordinary "carte de visite," swimming in a pickle bottle full of whale oil, was offered for my acceptance. I grasped my trusty cudgel, and in tragic tones belched out, "Hence, horrible shadow, unreal mockery, hence!" and refused to touch the greasy concoction.

I refuse my portrait in oil.

The chairman thereupon muttered something as to its being impossible to apportion the gift amongst the subscribers, and asked me if I persisted in my refusal of the present.

"Keep it yourself," I cried to the chairman, who was a very bald man, "and oil your hair with it." He then rose and said that "that idea of the poet's suggested another to his mind. It was," he remarked, "an ancient custom in the East to anoint their prophets, priests, and kings," and he thought the honour might appropriately be extended to modern poets, concluding a long oration by calling on some one in the audience to volunteer as poetical anointer for the *nonce*.

Quick as thought, one of the bold villians collared the bottle and approached me, but before he got the bung extracted I was on guard, and we wrestled up and down the room, the oil scattering over the entire audience, not a single soul being able to escape. As the gas had by this time been screwed out, I left the place under cover of the darkness, minus my hat and stick; but consoled myself with the idea that the garments of these jokers suffered more from splashes of oil than mine did.

That night, at a farewell symposium at Paton's Lane, Michael Kinchley, with tears in his eyes, implored me to reconsider my decision as to going to Perth.

"Michael," I said more in sorrow than in anger, "What has my life been in Dundee ever since I emerged from the obscurity of carpet weaving? Listen! I have written poems, of which the most distinguished **A retrospect.** critic of the century said, 'Shakespeare never wrote anything like this.' I sold these poems at the price of indifferent herrings—six for twopence. In these and other ways, both by precept and example, I have constantly endeavoured to raise the morality of the people of Dundee to the level of common depravity. These are the services; what has been the reward? I asked for bread, and they gave me a stone—not 14 lbs., Michael. At every meeting I have attended I have been taken home wounded. If I refused to go I lost my living. If I went I was half murdered. In a word, refusal meant neglect and poverty;

attendance, rotten eggs and a few coppers—which superabundant means of livelihood the authorities have now stopped. Think of it, Michael, and now say if you really think I should stay?"

"The will of the Lord be done, Willie," was Michael's pious termination of the argument.

I am invited to Downfield.
I should have started for Perth next day, but the morning's post brought me a letter from Downfield asking me to come out to that village next evening to receive a parting gift. The writer, evidently a man of culture, stated that my many friends and admirers there had from time to time heard with feelings of intense indignation of the unparalleled indignities which had been heaped on me in Dundee: indignities and atrocities which made them profoundly thankful that they were not an integral part of that adjacent and barbarous community, whose moral atmosphere none but drunkards, thieves, and liars could breathe with impunity, and whose cup of iniquity now overflowed by its treatment of a man so unique in the history of the world as to stagger humanity of the moral type such as is to be found on the banks of the classic Dighty; a river he implored me to immortalise at the next attack of the poetical "meagrims."

The present, I was informed, was to take the shape of a watch and chain and a substantial supper.

This letter fairly charmed me; but I was too busy packing for Perth to reply, a neglect which was remedied by my man-of-iron friend, who, as I before mentioned was a very good poet for an amateur. He wrote to Downfield with great acceptance there as follows:—

"To-morrow night, if all be right,
 Be sure I'll come your airth;
The watch and chain I'll aye retain,
 And tak' the rest to Perth."

In due time I arrived. The supper consisted of bread and cheese, of which I partook very heartily. After this dry and homely repast, the presentation took place. However, to make a long story short, the chain was a penny steel one, and the watch was only the case of one made of pinchbeck, with not the vestige of a wheel inside. I had faith this time; but if faith without works be dead, verily a watch without works is deader. This was the last straw, and it fully reconciled me to my translation to the fair city.

CHAPTER XI.

I go to Perth and Visit Inverness.

And in praise of thee I must say
I never received better treatment in my day
Than I received from my admirers in bonnie Inverness,
This upon my soul and conscience I do confess.—*M'Gonagall.*

THIS chapter then finds me and Mrs M'Gonagall ensconced in a humble but fairly clean garret in South Street, in the ancient and historical capital of Scotland. How restful and calm everything seemed to us after the storm and strife of Dundee, a town I shall never enter again, unless I lose my senses or am carried thither by force. This I have vowed on my bended knees, and the resolution is unalterable.

The circumstances which led to the adoption of this drastic action on my part are interesting, and well worthy of setting down with my usual lucid and veracious detail.

It was a beautiful September evening, just about sunset, in 1894. I had had a most encouraging and successful day amongst the shopkeepers of Perth, who one and all of them had treated me with an entire absence of that bear-baiting, so common with their class in Dundee. I was wending my way homewards from Bridgend, and when about the middle of that substantial structure—once par excellence the Tay Bridge, which, when over a hundred years old, laughed to scorn the storm which wrecked its two-year-old usurper in Dundee—I was accosted by a Dundee gentleman well known to me for many years.

"Good evening, poet," was his familiar greeting. "How are you liking Perth."

"Good evening, sir," I replied, shaking his outstretched hand. "Who would not like a city like this? Look around you anywhere, and you see a fit and natural setting for a poet."

"It is certainly very pretty," he said somewhat indifferently.

"Pretty?" I exclaimed. "If you had been a poet you would have said it is glorious! sublime!! perfect!!! I myself never saw anything like it, not even in America; as for Dundee" ——

"Stop, Mr M'Gonagall, stop," he interrupted. "You feel sore about Dundee, and I don't wonder at it; but do you recollect who wrote those magnificent lines, the refrain of which is 'most gorgeous to be seen, near to Dundee and the Magdalene Green.' I am afraid," he continued, "it's not the scenery of Dundee which annoys you; but I think and hope that that will be all right by and bye. I have reason to believe that the magistrates are sorry that, through an unfortunate misunderstanding, a rupture has occurred in the friendly relationship which used to subsist between you. They are also sorry that no *modus vivendi* is in the circumstances at all possible, seeing that if they apologised, it would be a palpable acknowledgment of wrong done to you, which would endanger their seats at the ensuing and every subsequent November until the whole 'bally board' was abolished."

Regrets of the Dundee Magistrates.

"Sir," I asked, "are you duly authorised to say all this on their behalf?"

"Never mind that meantime," said the gentleman with a peculiar leer on his cockle eye; "but you can put me down as an unaccredited emissary if you like. But look here; suppose I brought you a full apology, would you agree to burn that apology in my presence immediately after its perusal, and then resume the *statu quo ante bellum.*"

"No, sir," I ejaculated vehemently. "There must be no miserable subterfuges of this sort, they must apologise from the very house tops. And to complete the *entente cordiale*, after procuring a perpetual pass for the Newport Railway, they must ride with me in an open carriage through Dundee. To spare their feelings as much as possible, I am content to waive the question of indemnity. They need not be apprehensive of a loss of dignity in fulfilling these conditions, for the poet is greater than the magistrate, and justice must be done, if the heavens should fall. This, sir, is my ultimatum." With that we parted.

My magnanimity.

To this there was no reply, verbal or written, official or non-official, although months have elapsed since our interview. In these circumstances, and as I am getting fairly well fed, my manhood and the dignity pertaining to my sacred calling of a duly ordained poet compels me to declare the incident finally closed, and to proclaim to all whom it may concern that it cannot under any circumstances be re-opened.

Before I relegate the matter to the limbo of oblivion, I can only say that Dundee must now suffer for its magistrates, even as they must suffer for me. This is no threat, it is simply the poet's "anathema maranatha," and a deeply injured man's last word regarding it.

With reference to Perth itself I have nothing to say against it, except that after about eight months experience I found it too small for me to earn a living in, after the first newness of my advent amongst its inhabitants had worn off. What little I latterly earned there was not, however, at the peril of life and limb, as in Dundee. Had the Fair City been as populous as the city of Jute my lamentations would have ceased, and this chapter would have been, with the exception of Glasgow, an exception to the foregoing ten; but the malign influence of the stars still pursued me, and starvation and I got more intimately acquainted than ever.

Resolve to go to Edinburgh.
In these circumstances, we determined to migrate to Edinburgh. Like a hare, I had run my course, only to return to end it where I started; for by this time I had firmly resolved to leave my ashes in the metropolis of Scotland, to which place I had had of late not a few calls from the students of its ancient University, in which a chair of poetry for me was spoken of. But more of that anon.

In Perth, bar the starvation, I was fairly fortunate, and will ever remember it with comparative pleasure. For one thing, one of the greatest compliments I ever received was during my stay here. It was from a shopkeeper in the city, who knew what he was talking about. He told me that he was an ardent lover of poetry, and read everything in that shape he could come across. "Look here, poet," he said. "I do not wish to flatter any man before his face, it is against my creed; but common honesty and a sense of fairplay compels me to say that your poems are unique. In Scott, Byron, or Burns, for instance, if you omit a line, ten to one you lose the sense. With you it is totally different. I have read a whole production of yours, omitting each alternate line, and geting quite as much sense and literary power out of it as ever."

"Nay, more, if you read the fourth line first, and work back, the effect is quite as wonderful. The other night my wife pointed out to me that, in experimenting with a recent issue, she managed to derive even more benefit from it by reading the last line first, the first line next, the penultimate line third, the second line fourth, and so on till its natural conclusion by exhaustion."

"With this one I have bought just now we are to try another experiment to-night. We mean to clip out each word separately, shake them all up in a bag, and paste them together on a clean sheet of paper as they come, and will let you know the result. If it is as I anticipate, I would strongly advise you to take out a patent, and float it in £1 shares 'The Patent Reversible Poetry Company (Limited),' in which I would be glad to invest as a shareholder."

I decline commerce. I thanked the gentleman cordially, but told him that such commercial enterprises were not at all in my line; but that I would gladly supply the raw material, and sell him the patent rights for a consideration, if the result of his next trial justified his anticipations. At our next interview he told me that "the test was too severe even for my effusions, so that meantime at least the matter would go no farther." At the same time, he assured me that both he and his good lady fully agreed that the individual words were fully up to the Shakespearean standard, the only difference discernible in the completed article consisting merely in the matter of their arrangement.

During my stay in Perth also, two remarkable and outstanding events in my career occurred—red letter happenings—the happy memory of which I will carry till my dying day. The first brought me a glorious outing, a splendid feast, and a considerable quantity of coin, and the second a knightood, which placed me socially above Burns, and just a little lower than Scott.

I will describe them both—not the poets, but the events. The first is my famous trip to Inverness. Know then that in answer to numerous petitions, both oral and unspoken, the morning of the 15th of October, 1894, had not long dawned when the peculiar, business-like, rat-a-tat-tat of the postman startled our hearts with a flutter of hopeful excitement. "There's a letter, Willie," said my better half. "I houp there's siller in't frae somebody or ither;" but her face suddenly clouding at the recollection of how our home at Paton's Lane used to look liker a bank than a bunk with inconvertible cheques; she added more deliberately, "But I hope it's no a sham cheque again." I went to the door, got the letter, and opened it. It ran thus:—

GILLION'S HOTEL,
INVERNESS, *October 14th 1894.*

Most Miraculous Minstrel,

As chairman of the "Heather Blend Club," I am directed by the members of that august body to solicit the honour of your patronage and presence at our annual dinner, which takes place at the above hotel on the evening of the 16th inst. You are requested to come in Highland costume, and in case your accoutrements are in need of some slight repairs, I enclose you five shillings in stamps. This sum will in no way prejudice the silvery collection you will receive here in person.

Your appearance on the Inverness platform, by the train leaving Perth at 10 A.M., will be a sufficient acceptance of this cordial invitation.—Yours truly, A. GOSSIP.

P.S.—Show this letter to the authorities at Perth Station, and it will pass you to Inverness and back. A.G.

"It's anither 'cod,' Willie," cried my wife with an unmistakable ring of conviction in her tones. "The stamps is a' richt, and 'am thankful for them; but a' the rest o'd, believe me, is a regular 'cod.'"

I was not very sure myself, for if any man's experience ever shattered his faith in humanity, that experience was mine. So, reaching for my hat and stick, I said, "I'll soon put the matter beyond conjecture by a visit to the station."

"Man, Willie, that's a sensible idea. Tak' the stamps wi' you, and get the stationmaster to gae you the five shillings for them. He'll maybe do that for you, whether it's a cod or no," she added, "for I can tell you my accoutrements, as that wag ca's them, is michty sair oot o' repair as weel as your ain."

My visit to the station was satisfactory in every way, and so with a heart to match my stomach for lightness, I returned to South Street, and sent Mrs Mac. shopping in order to procure what would afford to me at least ample practice for the big burst to-morrow.

"It may be a' richt," the wife said, as loth to depart from her preconceived notion of a "cod;" "but I'll believe it better when you come back wi' a hail skin an' a pund or twa o' cauld beef i' your pooch."

By this time my doubts had fairly fled, and punctually at 10 A.M. on the 16th, in splendid spirits, I steamed out of the station, and in due course ran through Murthly, Dunkeld, Pitlochry, and the finest Highland scenery in the world, arriving in Inverness up to time, to find the gentleman waiting me at the station.

He was a tall, powerful, handsome man, whose genial manners and perfect courtesy at once put me perfectly at ease. He escorted me to the hotel, where he introduced me to the landlord, who told me in a very hearty way to order what I liked, and when I liked, as long as I stayed at his hotel. As I was hungry, I took full advantage of this *carte blanche*, and ordered and dispatched to two cups of coffee the largest, thickest and best beef steak I ever saw, even in dreams.

Two hours after this dinner was served, and the members (a goodly crew) as well as myself did ample justice to the good things provided. In brief, it was the best dinner, the best company, the best programme, and the best collection for me I ever saw, with the single exception of my Glasgow affair. The principal items in the programme were "Bannockburn" and "The Rattling Boy from Dublin Town," my singing of which brought tears of laughter to the eyes of every one. I had a splendid bed all to myself—no Fetter Lane chums this time—a sumptuous breakfast, a luncheon in my pocket, and the mighty remains of a huge roast to carry home; Mr Gossip parting with me at the station the happiest man in all the land.

But why need I describe all this in plain prose, when I did it so much better in one of the very finest poems I ever wrote. It runs thus. Kindly read it carefully, as I have one or two comments to make upon it :—

'Twas on the 16th of October, in the year 1894,
I was invited to Inverness, not far from the sea shore,
To partake of a banquet prepared by the " Heather Blend
Gentlemen who honoured me without any hubbub. [Club,"

The banquet was held in the Gillion Hotel,
And the landlord, Mr McPherson, treated me right well;
Also the servant maids were very kind to me,
Especially the girl that polished my boots most beautiful to see.

The banquet consisted of roast beef, potatoes, and red wine,
Also hare soup and sherry and grapes most fine,
Also baked pudding and apples lovely to be seen,
Also rich sweet milk and delicious cream.

Mr Gossip, a noble Highlander, acted as chairman;
And when the banquet was finished the fun began,
And I was requested to give a public entertainment,
Which I gave, and it pleased them to their hearts content.

And for my entertainment they did me well reward,
By titling me there the "Heather Blend Club" bard;
Likewise I received an illuminated address,
Also a purse of silver, I honestly confess.

Oh, magnificent city of Inverness,
And your beautiful river, I must confess,
With its lovely scenery on each side,
Would be good for one's health there to reside.

There the blackbird and mavis together doth sing,
Making the woodlands with their echoes to ring
During the months of July, May, and June,
When the trees and the shrubberies are in full bloom.

And to see the river Ness rolling smoothly along,
Together with the blackbird's musical song,
When the sun shines bright in the month of May,
Will help to drive dull care away.

And Macbeth's castle is grand to be seen,
Situated on Castle Hill, which is beautiful and green;
'Twas there Macbeth lived in days of old,
And a very great tyrant he was, I am told.

I wish the members of the "Heather Blend Club" every
Hoping God will prosper them and bless; [success,
Long may Dame Fortune smile upon them,
For all of them I have met are kind gentlemen.

And in praise of them, I must say
I never received better treatment in my day
Than I received from my admirers in bonnie Inverness,
This upon my soul and conscience I do confess.

And now gentle reader, I will give you an object lesson regarding the peculiarities of my poetry, so eloquently referred to in a previous part of this chapter by my Perth shopkeeper friend and his lady. I refer, of course, to the reversible, interchangeable, double-breasted, universal-jointed nature of my compositions. This is the distinguishing mark of my work, to copy which is moral felony. Take, for instance, the first stanza of that poem on Inverness, which you have just read. Like the rock we used **The reversible** to buy at the fairs, break it where you will, **nature of** the hall mark of excellence stares you in the **my poetry.** face. Read the lines in any order you like: begin at the top, middle, or bottom, and continue in any direction you choose, and you receive the same benefit; or, take a little gum, and paste it gently on the back of the complete stanza, cut each word carefully out with a pair of fine scissors, then throw the lot against the wall, as you have seen a conjuror do with a pack of cards, and if you do not get the same result as by an ordinary straight forward reading, you have not manipulated according to directions. With sufficient practice the veriest novice could in time produce the most astounding piece of wall writing since the days of Belshazar, and quite as easily deciphered.

Byron, in describing that event, says "The king was on his throne, the satraps thronged the hall," which I must admit is a good enough description of a chairman at a meeting; but it must be patent to the meanest intelligence that that line lacks the directness, the poetical vividness, and force of my portrayal of an event of the same nature as described in the poem under review. "Mr Gossip, a noble Highlander, acted as chairman."

The longer I regard these things, the more sympathy I seem to have with a remark of another Perth admirer, who assured me that he could not stand anything in the poetry line between Shakespeare and myself; in which predicament I fearlessly assert Lord Byron stands, aye, and a host of others, both dead and alive, I could name, but for obvious reasons will not.

Why is it, I wonder, that even red letter days, like my outing at Inverness, are so alloyed with after effects as to turn out positive curses, instead of blessings in disguise? Why, after the lapse of so many years, for instance, do I so often devour that delicious dinner in delightful dreams, only to be awakened from them by the prosaic shout, "Willie, get up, your porridge is ready!"

My joys, with the exception of Glasgow, leave all alloyed.

That's the worst of these occasional bursts, they are apt to lessen one's appreciation of the daily food which lies easily within the reach of his means. Byron and Tennyson got bigger bursts than my Gillion Hotel fare every day, but enjoyed them no better than an economical German mechanic does the smell of a greasy rag, which is the only lunch my means are too often capable of reaching.

There is something rotten in the state of Denmark. What is it? and shall I ever find it out? The Good Book says, "The way of the transgressor is hard." I some times doubt it. "Wisdom above riches" is the motto of our order of the White Elephant; but with all deference to King Thebaw, he might have given me a little of the latter in exchange for a considerable quantity of the former which I sent him, as we shall see in the next chapter.

CHAPTER XII.

I am made a Knight of the White Elephant of Burmah.

> Grassmarket born, Grassmarket reared,
>   And yet he rose to be
> A bard who nearly twice appeared
>   At Courts of Royalty.—"*Court Circular.*"

THE venue of my life story is now changed farther away than even New York, to the land of burning suns, to the country of the elephant and the ruby, to the Andaman Islands, which are under the sway of that dusky, but powerful potentate, King Thebaw of Burmah. 'Tis a wonderful story, how our names came to be linked together, and reads more like a "Monte Christo" romance than the plain, unvarnished truth, which it undoubtedly is.

King Thebaw then sat in state in one of these islands. He sat on his gold and ivory throne. At either side of him was a huge elephant, life size, cast in solid silver. Right over his head gleamed a canopy of gold, surmounted by a wonderous peacock, whose body and tail were studded with diamonds and rubies as big as French beans. His royal robes shimmered with oriental pearls, like the firmament on a starry night.

The splendour of the scene beggars all description. The walls of the throne room in which he held his Court were of the purest white marble, relieved with tiers of vivid green, gothic shaped niches all round, from the topaz inlaid floor to the massive gold dome, so richly set with emeralds. In many of these niches were statues of men in gold, mounted on silver elephants. These statues were those of the Knights of the White Elephant of Burmah since the flood, an Order open to merit alone wherever found. In former times these niches were strictly reserved for the poets of Burmah; but the rule was relaxed in consequence of a fear which had for some generations possessed the Rulers of Burmah of not being able to fill all the blanks with native talent before the year of our Lord 2000. This limit was set by the founder of the Order, with the prophetic intimation if it was exceeded, with one single niche left untenanted, the Empire of Burmah would crumble into oblivion.

Rules of the Order of the White Elephant.

The hall was thronged by men gorgeously attired, of every nationality under heaven. It was the annual meeting of the Knights of the Holy Order, convened to elect a worthy occupant for one of these much coveted recesses in the wall. Right opposite the king, at the extreme end of the hall, stood another throne, scarcely less magnificent than the one on which Thebaw sat. This was and is the chair of the Holy Order, in which the duly elected knights—men of outstanding ability in the realms of poetry—are in the fulness of time installed with all the rights and ceremonies prescribed by the illustrious founder.

For seven long years none had been found worthy of instalment, or else were in some way or other unable to fulfil the strictly-imposed conditions, and so the king was sad, sullen, and morose. The harpers who harped on silver harps, and the trumpeters who trumpeted on golden trumpets, tried in vain to bring a smile to the sulky monarch's face. Let them play their liveliest music, the muscles on that mahogany frontispiece would not relax to the tenth of a hairsbreadth, and the only response elicited from it was a sigh and a groan, and a doleful "Ah, me." They varied the tune a dozen times, but all to no purpose, the stolid look became more impassive still, and a fearful funereal silence fell on all around.

At length a Scotsman, Macdonald by name, high in the Order, and poet Laureate of Burmah, was seen to whisper in the ear of the chief of the musicians. That functionary, with a wave of his hand, at once stilled the orchestra, then he in turn whispered something in the ear of each bandsman. After a longish pause, the music struck up again, and a sudden transformation took place. You have seen an icebound pool, suddenly kissed by a genial thaw, brake up in wrinkles and tears. This is a weak metaphor, and a feeble indication of what happened to the royal face. First he smiled—the first smile he had smiled for nearly two years— then he roared in a perfect paroxism of laughter, eventually rising on his throne and dancing like one possessed, the tears of mirth rolling in torrents down his ebony cheeks.

"Stop! stop!" he roared to the chief musician. "Stop, or I shall go mad with joy. In the name of all the Burmese gods at once, what tune is this?"

Then the poet Laureate opened his mouth and replied, "Sire,"

"It is the 'Rattling Boy from Dublin town,'
By a British bard of great renown."

"Bring him forth," was the royal mandate, "and see if we cannot get him to fill at least two niches; but, meantime," he continued, "let our chief singer sing me the words of this all too fascinating melody." At this command the Poet Laureate, first bowing to the king, and saying, "Sire, prefer to do justice to this myself," he nodded to the conductor, and straightway broke forth, to the accompaniment of the harps, the trumpets, and the cymbals—

"I'm the rattling boy from Dublin town,
I courted a girl called Biddy Brown;
Her eyes they were as black as sloes,
She had black hair and an aquiline nose.
  Wack fal the dooral, ooral, ido,
  Wack fal the dooral, ooral, aa',
  Wack fal the dooral, ooral, ido,
  Wack fal the dooral, ooral, aa'.

Now Biddy Brown, from County Down,
Was the biggest decayver in the town,
For all the time she was coortin' me
She was goin' about wid Barney M'Ghee.
  Wack fal the dooral, &c.

Till one fine day it came to pass
I met bould Barney wid my lass;
Wid my darling shileleagh I knocked him down—
For I'm the rattling boy from Dublin town.
  Wack fal the dooral, &c.

Said Barney M'Ghee unto me,
I must cave in, I plainly see;
So take you back your Biddy Brown,
The greatest decayver in Dublin town.
  Wack fal the dooral, &c.

> Then Biddy wid the aquiline nose,
> Punched poor Barney's as he rose;
> 'Farewell,' she cried, 'ye cowardly clown,
> I'm off wid my boy from Dublin town.'
>   Wack fal the dooral, &c."

And the Poet Laureate sang, and the orchestra played, and the king danced, and ever and anon as the music stopped or Macdonald paused for breath, the king shouted impatiently, "Go on, go on." Never was such a lively or a more exhausting jig danced, sung, or played since time began.

The dance of the gods. All this was duly minuted in the records of the Order, and the scene therein described as the "Dance of the Gods." At length the king, thoroughly tired out, had only strength enough to exclaim, "Let him fill three niches," when he collapsed.

On regaining consciousness, it was fully explained to him that the bard lived in Perth, Scotland, and a committee was appointed to draw up an intimation of his election to the Holy Order of the Knights of the White Elephant of Burmah, which intimation duly arrived at South Street towards the end of January, 1895.

In this letter—which was of enormous size, and addressed Sir Wm. Topaz Macgonagall—was a real silver elephant, attached to a green silk ribbon, which I understand is the insigna of the knighthood. The letter itself is as follows:—

COURT OF KING THEBAW,
ANDAMAN ISLANDS, *December 2nd, 1894.*

Dear and Most Highly
   Honoured Sir,

Having the honour to belong to the same Holy Order as yourself, I have been requested to inform you by His Royal Highness King Thebaw that you, after satisfactory examination through the medium of one of your own immortal songs, have been duly elected a Grand Knight of the Most Holy Order of the White Elephant of Burmah (three niches), and that henceforth you are to be known and respected as Sir William Topaz M'Gonagall, G.K.H.O.W.E.B. That you will consent to accept of the high honour now offered to you is the wish nearest to the hearts not only of the king himself, but also of all your countrymen here in the East, who will never cease to pray that you may be long spared to enrich British literature by your grand and thrilling works, the power and pathos of which have been so exhaustively tested at this Court.

Should you see fit to do the ancient Kindom of Burmah the honour of accepting the ribbon of its highest award, you will kindly pay its capital a visit at your earliest convenience, to be duly installed in the holy chair of the Knights of the above Order, from which you will be expected, according to the custom of the holy fraternity, to address a manifesto to the whole world.

King Thebaw, who has been terribly impressed by your extreme modesty, will not risk insulting your sensitive feelings by offering you any filthy lucre, more especially as the shield and motto of the Order is a white elephant wading to the belly in gold, with the legend "Wisdom above Riches."

At the same time, as a signal mark of unusual appreciation, he is sending you by an early steamer the biggest white elephant in all Burmah, as a living and standing reminder to you of the colossal nature of the honour he has bestowed upon you.

I have the honour to be, most noble and illustrious sir, your most humble brother in the fraternity of the poets,

C. MACDONALD, K.O.W.E.B.,
Poet Laureate of Burmah.

By order of His Royal Highness the King.

TOPAZ GENERAL.
TOPAZ MINISTER.
SECRETARY OF STATE.
HOLDER OF SEALS.
KEEPER OF THE WHITE ELEPHANT.

P.S.—Kindly address all communications *re* this and other matters of State to Sylvester Smith, Esq., Burmese Charge d'Affaires, 21 Gardners' Crescent, Edinburgh.

Mixed feelings. This letter filled me at once with the keenest pleasure and the greatest consternation—pleasure to have my services recognised by a knighthood, and absolute terror at the coming of that enormous brute, which, even if carriage paid, would devour in an hour all that I could earn in a month, and keep me in perpetual starvation.

Thus my pleasures by a perverse fate have always been alloyed. Besides, where was I to keep the monster? If it attempted to reach my garret in South Street, at every step the stairs would go like rotten girds, and the damages I would have to pay would totally overwhelm me. If I led it about the streets the police would interfere, and no stable in Perth has a doorway sufficiently big to admit it. I do not know the value of such an animal; but this I do know, that motto of the Order or no motto, I would much rather have had half of the gold it is depicted as wading among than twenty elephants. Of course, I dare not say this to Thebaw, or he might deem me unworthy of the knighthood.

I am nervous and sinful. To such a state of nerves was I reduced that, sinful man that I am, I prayed fervently that the ship which conveyed it to me would become a total wreck. Of course, I would have preferred that the brute should jump overboard and be drowned; but if that was not to be, I was prepared, rather than face that elephant in Perth, to read with equanimity the account of the whole bally lot, captain, crew, and passengers, being engulfed in the bosom of any sea, red, black, or white, so long as the elephant went with them.

That night I dreamed a dream, and the interpretation thereof was not such as to tax the powers of a Daniel. I dreamed I lay, in the brilliant sun of a July day, in a lovely meadow dotted with daisies and buttercups, that I was being crowned with garlands and loaded with honours, and acclaimed as the king of poetry, and so loud were the plaudits of the people that I could not hear the stealthy approach of a gigantic form, which anon assumed the shape of an enormous elephant, which presently lay down beside me, imprisoning my legs tightly under its huge haunches. By and bye it rolled more and more over me, till its weight was so oppressive as to threaten me with complete annihilation. I wriggled in a vain endeavour to escape, only to find my face in close proximity to its glaring eyes and terrible tusks ready to gore my breathless body. At this I awoke in an agony of fear and sweat, and narrated the dream to my alarmed spouse.

"Ah, Willie," she said, "is this no most michty? It's the worst calamity ever cam' ower you! A sham cheque disna eat onything, it's juist a 'cod' an' dune we'd, an' a pepperin' at an entertainment cleans aff or heals in a fortnicht; but this brute— an' they say they live 300 year—'ill be a bonny millstane roond yer neck day an' nicht a' yer life, unless ye pushion it as sune's it comes."

My worst calamity.

"That's all very well," I said; "but what would the king think? He might revoke my knighthood"

"Weel, weel," she said, "juist lat him du'd; there's nae siller comin' we'd, an' if that's the case, he micht as weel gi'en ye a nicht-cape as a nicht-hood, an' a hantle better too, for the ane wad be some use, and the ither, as far as I can see, michty little."

What was the use of arguing with a woman possessed of ideas like these, so, with a deep drawn sigh, I was once more flung on my own resources. These inspired me to write at once to Mr Sylvester Smith, in Edinburgh, as follows:—

> South Street, Perth, *Jan. 31, 1895.*
>
> Dear Sir,—The knighthood is to hand. Tell the king from me I thank him with my whole soul, and will write him in due course; but for heaven's sake tell him to stop that elephant he is sending me anywhere between Burmah and Perth. If you do not, my blood lies at your door, for the moment it reaches Perth my life is not worth an hour's purchase.—Yours truly and in trepidation, William M'Gonagall, Poet.

In due time I was plunged into the third heaven of delight by a telegram from Edinburgh, brief, but blissful—

From Smith, Edinburgh.
To M'Gonagall, Perth.
"Elephant stopped in Suez Canal."

I rushed upstairs to my wife as fast as I could from the post office, where I got it, and entering the house breathless, I shouted, flourishing the wire, "Hurrah! hurrah! the elephant has been stopped in the Suez Canal."

"Dear me, Willie," ejaculated my astonished spouse. "Dear me, what an enormous brute that soo must hae been to swallow an elephant; nae winder it stuck in the brute's gullet or canal, as they ca' it. Lat it get oot o'd the best wey it can, it's better there than in Perth ony wy."

You can easily conceive the difficulty of enlightening one who, in culinary and general domestic arrangements is all that could be desired, but whose knowledge of that great waterway was so evidently limited.

As I learned afterwards, the moving mountain was booked at Burmah *carriage forward*. You can form some little idea of the immense load which was lifted from my chest, more especially when I tell you that the Khedive of Egypt, into whose hands it eventually fell, had to pay £200 for food and carriage, and to name it "M'Gonagall" before he was allowed to touch it. Relieved from this incubus I breathed freely, so freely that existence, even in poverty and as far in debt as they would allow me, was positively delicious. It was only occasionally in dreams after this that I suffered from "Elephantophobia." These fears, however, entirely vanished in waking moments, and I wrote a letter the king, which ran thus :—

South Street, Perth, *March 10th, 1895.*

To His August Majesty the King of Burmah.

Sire,—This comes greeting from your humble slave, the Poet M'Gonagall, on whom your Majesty has vouchsaved the light of your countenance by creating him a worshipful Knight after the Order of the White Elephant, whose motto, I am proud to note, is "Wisdom above Riches." May both be multiplied to your Royal Highness until your storehouses of each are abundantly filled.

In the case of your humble slave, nature and circumstances have made a very one-sided arrangement as regards those two precious commodities ; for at the present I can say without fear of contradiction, if the wisdom of your humble slave were not above the riches he possesses, he would indeed be, what the whole world knows he is not, the veriest idiot in the universe. I am not complaining, only had it been otherwise I would not have been forced to forgo the greatest pleasure the world has ever dangled before my wistful eyes. I refer to your Royal Highness's unique and powerful present, which I did not countermand for any other reason save that I could neither pay carriage on it or feed it any way, let alone in accordance with the manner I would desire to do, for the reverence and love which I bear for the august donor, whose large hearted benevolence to the poor and needy is well known all over the civilised globe.

"Your Highness's early reply,
Will raise its recipient heavens high."

Your abject and grateful slave,

Sir WILLIAM TOPAZ M'GONAGALL, G.K.H.O.W.E.B.

This, as was fitting, was the first time I signed my new title, not excepting my letter to the Charge d'Affaires, to whom under cover I sent the foregoing; but I never received a reply owing, I understand, to a revolution which took place in Burmah in consequence, I am informed, of the fact that a three-niched honour—the first for 1000 years—had been conferred on a foreigner.

I leave Perth and come to Edinburgh. This, though excessively disappointing, was nothing exceptional to my usual luck, and so, with an empty purse, an empty stomach, and a no less empty title, I, William M'Gonagall, to be known henceforth as Sir William Topaz M'Gonagall, left Perth, and took up my abode in Edinburgh.

CHAPTER XIII.

I go to Edinburgh.

*'Tis the sunset of life gives me mystical lore,
And coming events cast their shadows before.—Campbell.*

NONE but a poet can adequately sympathise with the feelings of a poet returning to the place of his nativity to die. That sublime thought occurred to me in ruminating over the fact that Sir Walter Scott did precisely the same thing, and returned, even as I did, to leave his ashes in the city which we claim in common as "Mine own romantic town."

When the sunset of life has been reached, when the allotted span has been passed, when the sand glass has almost run down, and life's fitful fever is nearly over, what a serious and melancholy pleasure it is to the sensitive and cultured mind of the poet to know that his bones, after so many aches and wanderings, will rest their eternal rest in the place where he was born.

Many people attach but little importance to this, but of a surety their minds must have been cast in coarser moulds than those of the Baronet bard and poet Knight of sweet Edina.

I have often thought that in many respects besides this, we two were similarly circumstanced. I do not for a moment mean in the matter of public appreciation, and the luxuries which that appreciation brings. Without comparing our respective abilities, his success was less on account of these abilities than the suitability of their particular trend to the tastes of the people. They had been long educated to ballad poetry, which, without in any way deprecating, is not exactly in conformity with my ideas of what is best for the moral elevation of the masses. Be that as it may, however, his predecessors in the muses found this kind of thing as little in demand as mine is now; but they had pioneered the business, till it became as familiar in the mouths of the people as household words, and Scott was wise enough to step in and reap the reward.

Ballad poetry good enough in its way.

Pioneering, as I have found out, is a hungry job, for poetry is not like steam or electricity, the new style does not at once supercede the old, and allow the poet to make his fortune right away. No; some other fellow comes along when he is dead, continues his strain, and goes off with the dollars. That is why Abbotsford was a more palatial residence than the one I found in Potter Row.

But this is not exactly what I mean to convey as to our being in many respects similarly circumstanced. It consists rather in these things:—We both loved Edinburgh with an intensity unknown to the denizens of any other city; we both believed ardently in our great poetic attainments; we both, as already stated, longed to return to mix our dust with the kindred clay of dear Auld Reekie; and we both had practical and prosaic, rather than pensive and poetical partners.

I am told that on one occasion at Abbotsford, on Scott pointing out to his wife the lambs with their dams sporting and frisking in the bright May sunshine, and exclaiming "Are they not splendid?" he was horrified at the good lady's unexpected but totally innocent response, "Yes, dear, with mint sauce." This was so like my good lady's remarks, as we sat the first day of our arrival in Princes Street Gardens. It was a beautiful afternoon in spring, the sunlight was streaming on Scott's monument, the Castle, the Calton Hill, and all the "palaces and towers," which so fascinated Burns, and makes this scene so ravishingly romantic, that the tears started to my eyes as I enthusiastically exclaimed, "Is there a fairer spot on earth?"

Similarity between Sir Walter's wife and mine.

"It's guid enough, Willie," said my companion, "but naething to mak' a sang aboot. I was thinkin' mair aboot hoo we were genna get meat. We canna live on scenery, an' up till noo we hivna lived michty fat on poetry. Geid up man a' thegither, an' try an' get a job as a licht porter or even as a sandwich man, an' lat's hae a regular set wage, though it's sma'. Scott, ower there," she continued, "had to chuck the poetry, and write his havers without clinkin' them, an' as I've heard ye say yersel, it peyed him far better."

Annoyed and indignant, I could not help being struck and consoled at the point she made in calling to my mind that Scott had really deserted the muses for the realms of fiction, which possibly accounted for the prophetic genius of poetry not paying him a visit, as she did to me, knowing as she did that I would stick to my colours through thick and thin, and that he would not.

I think, discerning reader, that this scores a point in favour of the Knight as against the Baronet; at all events it turned my wavering resolution into adamant, and so I told my wife that I would persevere even unto the end.

"Weel, weel, Willie, sin' ye took up that poetry craze ye've been a most obstinate brute of a man; but," she continued, "if ye winna be ruled by me in this maitter, what aboot that Chairge o' Affairs man at Gairner's Crescent? He micht do something for's. Eh, man! if his maister had only sent a stirk or a puckle sheep there wad a been some sense in'd; but an"——

"Hush, woman," I interrupted, "the man's maister, as you call him, is a king and a poet, and should be spoken about with more reverence."

"Michty me," she exclaimed excitedly, "that accoonts for'd noo. Ah, Willie, Willie! little did I think when I wis laundrymaid at Wast Green that I wad never till my dyin' day get a chenge o' my surroondings. Me that's haen so muckle experience o' them, baith indoor an' oot. I micht a kent he was a poet, or he never wad hae sent an elephant to a man 'at cudna feed a canary."

Being accustomed to such talk, as well as to the process familiarly known as pouring water on a duck's back, I answered not a word, but resolved to call on Mr Sylvister Smith as soon as I got properly settled down at Potter Row, in the vicinity of Bristo. Potter Row, I may say in passing, bears not the slightest resemblance to Rotten Row in London, although if a fair swap of the names could be effected it would be to the obvious advantage of both, as there is more pottering about in the one, and much, very much, that is rotten about the other. It is, in fact, a fairly successful rival to the Grassmarket for

Potter Row and Rotten Row contrasted.

salubriousness, only it is much narrower. But whether this is an advantage or not is an open question.

Mark Twain, writing of a city he visited in Italy, says, "The streets are narrow and the smells are abominable; yet, on reflection, I am glad they are narrow. If they had been wider they would have held more smell, and killed all the people."

Having, however, been acclimatised to this sort of thing there was not so much danger. Scientists say that if you put a dozen of sparrows under a big glass globe, and exclude the air, they will go on living say for twenty minutes; but if you plump a fresh chap in at the end of twelve minutes or so, he will pop off his perch at once as dead as Queen Anne.

Say what you will, vitality is of more importance than environment, and the "Row" was decidedly the place to practice that in. For instance, I could have been removed from it to Abbotsford and have been not a whit the worse, whereas had the process been reversed, and Scott been compelled to reside in my single apartment, the awful fate of sparrow No. 13 would have been his inevitable doom. But I am again digressing.

The great opportunity of my life. Next day was one of my red letter days. I was well received, more especially by the students, who congregated round me in the quadrangle of the college, and cleared off at an average of twopence each all the poems I had brought with me. It was the one opportunity of a lifetime for a great poet, and I took full advantage of it. Young men, the future ministers and doctors of the world, trampling each other down in order to obtain that which they would masticate and assimilate before giving broadcast from the pulpit and at the bedside, to cheer drooping and hungry souls.

Though I was glad of the money, believe me the scene —which would have made a splendid picture—was to me its own reward. As soon as my supply was exhausted they lifted me on their shoulders, and carried me in triumph all round; *a fete* I would not so much have objected to, although it crushed my hat and deranged my garments, if they had not suddenly dropped me on the hard stones, and hurt me considerably, so that I had to limp home somewhat painfully. To show the Spartan in me, I successfully concealed all trace of damage, which was principally in one of my knees.

I was glad next morning, on meeting one of the young men, to learn that the injury was not inflicted through *malice prepense*; but was occasioned, immediately prior to the fall, by the advent on the square of a very prosaic and rather jealous professor, who had never had an ovation of the same kind himself. Asking and obtaining my address, handing me a shilling, and informing me that a deputation from the college on important business would wait on me at my residence that evening, he lifted his hat and passed on. How different from the rude vulgarity of Dundee, with its eternal "Hey, mannie, whaur's yer shuttle?"

Edinburgh courtesy contrasted with Dundee's vulgarity.

That night five students called at my room. The spokesman, a fine upstanding specimen, with a rich brogue, who revelled in the name of O'Halloreen, moved that, as there was scarcely standing room, an insufficient supply of chairs, and a lady present, an adjournment be made to more suitable premises round the corner. This was carried with acclamation, and the strength of the wooden stair leading to my chamber was as well tested in their exit as if the Khedive's "M'Gonagall" had danced a jig on it.

The motion for adjournment had evidently been pre-arranged, for on arriving at a restaurant in the vicinity of the South Side Theatre we found some fifty or sixty students ensconced in a large back parlour, drinking, and apparently waiting our arrival, which was greeted with vociferous cheering of "Long live our lyric king, the great Sir William." A dozen tumblers were at once proffered to me, and a dozen hearty voices shouting simultaneously cried, "Drink, poet, drink !! drink with me !!" This was another opportunity which I at once embraced.

I preach temperance to the students. "Gentlemen," I said as soon as I could obtain a hearing, "the true poet needs no drink to stimulate his inspiration, unless it be an inspiration from below which he invokes. I unwittingly transgressed once, but never again. The night after the lamentable lapse I had a dream, in which the genius frowned upon me, and with an angry gesture and a voice full of pity, said 'I love thee M'Gonagall; but never more be a votary of mine.' I briefly recapitulated to her the extenuating circumstances, and swore never again to disgrace a calling which, with all due deference to you, gentlemen, is the most exalted on earth.

'The vision smiled, and disappeared with noiseless tread,
She spoke not, but vanished, and that's all she said.'

But I knew that I was forgiven. But never again, gentlemen, never again."

The effect was marvellous. It was a word in due season, for more than one half of the company made a veritable penticost of the meeting by endorsing the declaration of one of their number, to the effect that after the present orgie in my honour, it would be chronicled on the tablets of their memory as the very last booze they had had.

The big Irishman was then elected to the chair, and in a few well chosen words, proposed that "the Chair of Poetry in the University, so soon to be vacant, be offered to the great M'Gonagall."

Why so soon to be vacant?" queried a pugnacious looking, thin faced chap, with a nose of the whelk-picker order.

"Simply because he must leave it, as a better man has turned up. If he refuses to go, I have a persuader here," the chairman replied firmly, laying a huge horse pistol on the table before him.

Then there was wild consternation in the room, missiles of divers kinds, hard, soft, and insanitary, were flying about, and like the serenading Tom cat on the roof when pelted from the adjacent windows, things were coming my way at last.

What a drop. It was Dundee all over again, only in an exaggerated form. I made a blind rush for the door, but was stopped unceremoniously, and huddled into a chair. Silence ensued, the chairman apologised, and said it was the work of a thoughtless few, who would be expelled the college on the morrow; but as all their coats were very much cleaner than mine, I refused to be appeased, said I wanted no chair at the price of a cold-blooded murder, and that I would leave them to throw things at each other without my all too effective intervention.

After a lot of angry talk from both sides of the table, a motion was put to the meeting that the present occupant of the chair of poetry be allowed to die a natural death, provided M'Gonagall would agree to become his successor. To this, at the request of the meeting, and to bring peace, I at length assented, and the matter was allowed to drop.

But there was a resurrection from the floor, which I certainly would not have stayed for, if the chairman had not at the moment handed the hat round for a collection. This, to do them justice, totalled over thirty shillings; but scarcely was I in full possession thereof than the refurbished weapons of war, doing duty over again, began to fly about with redoubled fury, and if directed at each other, with very indifferent success indeed.

Strange mixture of generosity and brutality.

At length I escaped in the confusion, incident on explanations being made to the proprietor, which were even less successful, and arrived home an unwounded, but by no means stainless knight.

There certainly was not much damage done in this case, as the pros and cons were about equal; but the moral and intellectual effects were far reaching, as such scenes when bruited abroad inflame the bear baiting and badger drawing instincts, which are after all deeper rooted in ordinary humanity than the love of the muses, and the groans of pelted and suffering creatures sweeter to their ears than the finest strains from the lyre of Apollo.

But I certainly expected better things from students, and had high hopes from this particular batch that "the expulsive force of the new emotion" of my poetry would have acted as a charm to soothe their savage and murderous breasts; but no, civilisation with them is only the thin vineer it is on the men of Dundee, and I suppose on everybody else, except poets.

I have repeatedly remarked that it was my ardent wish to leave my bones in Edinburgh. This yearning the students, and others infected by their example, did everything in their power to enable me to realise sooner than I desired.

Coming events cast their shadows before. Whether they have been successful I know not; but even as I write I have a strong premonition that the end is not far off, and if the people of Edinburgh have not been quite so gentle with me as my merits and disposition warranted, yet, to do them justice, they have been exceedingly generous. If they did treat me somewhat on the lines experienced by the certain man in Scripture when he fell among thieves, they never grudged the bandages, the oil, and the twopence, and were altogether in both rôles streets ahead of Dundee.

But why need I recapitulate. History repeats itself painfully often in my experience. If it has not been one thing, it has been another equally bad; even in Inverness and Glasgow, where the kindness and the coin went together, it had its drawbacks. 'Twas ever thus with me, and to tell how I emerged from one series of scrapes into another since my first appearance in public would fill ten large volumes. To recount one-half of my hairbreadth escapes would be to issue a treatise on providence; while to narrate a tithe of the rough handlings I received would form a second edition of the "Book of Martyrs."

In Dundee I had my skull fractured in a vile attempt to place me on the pedestal of the Burns statue. In Edinburgh I have on more than one occasion been three hours cleansing my garments from rotten eggs, ostensibly administered as an antidote to rotten egotism; in reality to gratify and excuse the promptings of the brute, of which I am hopeful they were more than half ashamed; but, still, unconquered and unconquerable as I lie, even on the confines of eternity, I have a greater opinion of my own merits than ever.

My opinion of my abilities unchanged to the very end.

I was in hopes that Mr Sylvester Smith might have made things a little easier for me; but, alas—my luck again—he was recalled to Burmah just one week before my appearance in Edinburgh. Whether his translation to the Far East was a calamity or not, I dare not, after my whole life's experience, venture to say, and I am afraid it is now too late to conjecture, for the land of Beulah looms nigh—that sunless realm, where every man is seen as he is, a heaven maybe to the poor poet, and a hell to the monarch and rich man who sneered at him here; a place where gold has not the potency of a god; where the first shall be last and the last first; the blessed Nirvana of eternal rest, where there is no starvation; the long longed for country of compensation, where there is nothing to hurt or destroy those who, like poor M'Gonagall, have already come through great tribulation.

CHAPTER XIV.

THE POET ATTENDS HIS OWN FUNERAL.

> Wafted from the spirit world,
> Still his emanations come;
> Where no missiles can be hurled,
> And the mockers' mouth is dumb.
> — *"The Unseen Sphere."*

COPY of a letter from a great admirer of the poet in Edinburgh to his life long *Fides Achales*, Michael Kinchley, in Dundee:—

POTTER ROW, EDINBURGH,
January 17th, 1905.

Dear Michael,

I have never seen you in the flesh, but have heard sufficiently about you from our mutual friend, the late Sir William M'Gonagall, to esteem you very highly. The deceased Knight of the White Elephant has often recounted to me as he sat at my fireside in this savoury region the wonderful David and Jonathan-like affection which existed between you. You appreciated him, and he appreciated your appreciation; that, I understand, was the bond betwixt you.

Our lodgings being reached by the same antique and risky entrance, I had ample opportunities afforded me of verifying on oath if necessary that the remembrance of your unique devotion touched him much, and comforted him mightily before he passed over.

An hour or so before that melancholy event took place he called softly to me, "Peter, I have been thinking very much to-day about my old and faithful friend, Michael Kinchley, in Dundee. Poor Michael," he continued faintly, "we had one or two rows, but for all that he aye thocht I was a great man, and I always knew he was right. What a pity it is that I cannot live long enough to see the world attain to Michael's standpoint. Mark me well, Peter, I do not on this solemn occasion wish to 'babble of green fields,' like the great Sir John, for I am lying on Pisgah, and can see the promised land of my fame very clearly, though, alas, to enter on its enjoyment has been denied me. Like the prophet leader of Israel, God knows where I am to be buried; but like him also, I trust I may in some way or other be permitted to give all whom it may concern some particulars of my death and funeral.

"It is a strange desire, is it not? but it is a strong one. I feel it here," he continued, touching his chest feebly with his emaciated right hand; "it burns, it consumes with a fiercer fervour than that flame which was once kindled in me long ago in Paton's Lane.

"In my life my name has been strangely linked with that of William Shakespeare, whom I have just, as it were, beaten on the post by being created a knight. But this triumph would sink into utter insignificance in the victory achieved by the gratifiation of the ardent longing I have now indicated. Besides, it would cheer poor Michael in the midst of his grief, and justify the unparalleled devotion with which he regarded me, to learn of this tardy recognition of my genius.

"I know it is an apparently unattainable desire, and yet something somehow tells me it will be realised.

Fancy what a facer it would be to my life-long enemies and the scoffers at my poetical inspiration if my name would go down to posterity as one of that unique trio who were able to give an account of their own obsequies, Moses, M'Gonagall, and Sherlock Holmes."

He added feebly, "It is a consumation devoutly to be wished," and so this strange and mighty man passed away, modest even in death, as shown by his quoting his last words; not from any of his own works, but from those of his mighty rival. Could magnanimity in mortal go farther than this? I weep, dear Michael, at its contemplation.

But I think I hear you saying, "Why did you not write and tell me all this before?" Wait a bit; there's a sequel, and a strange and eventful sequel it is, as you will surely admit. You know, or if you do not, know now that I am a spiritualistic medium, and attend seances in our own little circle of friends. Last night, at our meeting, the fact was communicated to me that the spook of a poet wished to interview me. My heart bounded, and my instinct at once told me who the inquirer was. It was, indeed, our mutual friend, M'Gonagall, the irrepressible, who, though dead, was yet speaking.

Immediately after mutual recognition I asked him, "Are you happy?" "Yes," came the laconic answer. "Why did you not seek me sooner," I queried. "Because for a long time," he replied, "I was seeking a connection with Michael; but he, poor chap, not being a spiritualist, I failed to find him, and I had no idea that you were in any way connected with the chosen people, until after much trouble and inquiry I eventually discovered the fact."

"Then your powers on the other side are limited like ours?" I asked.

"You are right, and you are wrong," was the rejoinder. "Our powers are limited, but not so circumscribed as yours. My time at the moment is, however, both limited and circumscribed; but before I come to the all-important question which is responsible for my presence here to-night, is there anything of more moment than matters of mere curiosity on which you would wish to be enlightened?"

"There is," I replied. "What position, for instance, do you occupy in your new sphere? Are you still a knight?"

The answer came, "There are neither kings, knights, or elephants here. The advancement on the astral plane is simply dependant on the start you get on earth. If there you have partaken of neither alcohol or beef you begin high right away, for this is indeed the land of compensation I so longed to reach, where the obscure mill lad or lass who struggled bravely to keep the widowed mother from want takes precedence of your Cæsars and Napoleons; a place where your hungerings and thirstings, ungratified on earth, are the only stepping-stones to penetrative knowledge of passing events on both sides, which is our only hall mark of greatness. I qualified so well in the body through stress of circumstances—which I foolishly deplored—that I knew from the moment I entered these regions everything that occurred with you, from a municipal squabble to the bursting up of an empire."

"Thanks, my dear poet." That reminds me, One more question and I am satisfied. "A friend of mine, a medium in Glasgow, wishes to know, but has hitherto been unable to ascertain, whether, in view of the obstructive and disgraceful tactics recently pursued in that city such a state of things is at all possible with you, and if *vox populi vox dei* is as great a travesty on truth on the other side as it is with us."

"I know to what you allude," was the prompt response, "and have carefully watched the developments of this case; but, judging from the tone of your question, I differ most entirely from the estimate your Glasgow friend has evidently formed of the principal actor in this interesting drama. The voice of the people is certainly the voice of God everywhere, more especially in Glasgow, where on more than one occasion I was fully appreciated, treated more than kindly, and applauded to the echo. I certainly am wholly and entirely in deepest sympathy with that doughty Scot, the municipal champion of the west, if for no other reason than that his character, circumstances, tenor, and general trend of intellect are precisely on all fours with my own.

"His persistent belief in himself almost equals mine, and he is quite as irrepressible. True, he is no poet.

"A yellow Primrose by a river's brim,
A yellow Primrose was to him
And nothing more."

Yet, nevertheless, I am fully persuaded that if King Thebaw had only known him, he would most assuredly have sent him long ere this two elephants and four niches in return for copies of his speeches to be read for aggravated offences by the inmates of his penal settlements. If these, together with my poetry, would not effect a reformation in Burmah, then God help that unhappy country."

"Thanks. One more question, poet. What about Shakespeare?" "Shakespeare," he said, "is still an undoubtedly great man. Three hundred and odd years ago he was awarded a palm in this place for that trite and true utterance of his, which still holds the philosophic field on both sides, 'There are more things in heaven and earth than are dreamed of in our philosophy.'

"Let that suffice, Peter, and seek to learn no more; but were I permitted I could a tale unfold which would make the rope, the razor, and the river your most beneficent institutions, nay, your universal methods for translation to this place. But that reminds me of my own departure. Know then and testify to all and sundry that I was present at my own funeral. I saw you there, like the last rose of summer left blooming well alone, not even Michael Kinchley in attendance.

"However, as far as that is concerned, I am satisfied, and although the cortege was not so numerous as a battalion, nor the mourning garments quite *a la mode*, yet as Shakespeare says regarding Laerte's wound, 'It was enough,' and my glimpse of it sufficient to enable me to take my place in the illustrious trio, as I so longed to do when I last saw you in the flesh.

"Eh! What? Which is the greater?" "No, not another word. Farewell, Peter; but, stay, "Tell

Michael that, in my own opinion, I am still a little ahead of Shakespeare,' inasmuch as while he was only awarded a palm, I, who surely supped my fill of earthly punishment, have fairly won 'A Martyr's Crown.'"

This *verbatum et liberatum* report I transmit to you in the full assurance that on its perusal you will be edified, built up, and comforted, nothing doubting as to the *bona-fides* of my strange narrative. The proof of its authenticity is overwhelming, and consists of the fact that twelve of the disciples of our order, all diligent seekers after truth, were present at the interview between Sir William and

Yours truly,

Peter A. Saphira.

The Editor of the "Lochee Lubricator" adds that on the very day on which Mr Kinchley received the foregoing he was heard by a neighbour reciting the *Nunc dimittis*, and found shortly thereafter placidly asleep with the portrait of the mighty man at his lips.

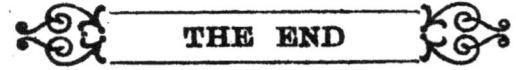

THE END

www.ingramcontent.com/pod-product-compliance
Lightning Source LLC
LaVergne TN
LVHW081357060426
835510LV00016B/1883